Your Infinite Power to Be Rich

Your Infinite

PARKER PUBLISHING COMPANY, INC., WEST NYACK, N. Y

Power to Be Rich

JOSEPH MURPHY, D.D., D. R. S., Ph.D., LL.D.
Fellow of the Andhra Research,
University of India

Reward Edition . . . . . January, 1973

Eleventh Printing . . . . . July, 1982

PRINTED IN THE UNITED STATES OF AMERICA

B & P

Also by the Author

Power of Your Subconscious Mind

Miracle of Mind Dynamics

The Amazing Laws of Cosmic Mind Power

How This Book Can Benefit You

This book is designed to be a very practical one. It is intended for men and women whose pressing need is for money, and who are seeking to claim the riches life has in store for them.

It is for those men and women who want immediate results and who are willing to put into application the simple down-to-earth techniques outlined in detail in this book. Within the following pages, you will find specific details and illustrations on the techniques to apply for getting riches as your natural way of life.

You can subscribe to the fundamental laws of the mind as explained in this book just as you would accept statements regarding laws and principles of electricity or mathematics as promulgated by an Edison, or an Einstein, and by applying them, get equally definite and certain results.

In writing this book, I have concentrated on plainness and simplicity of style, so that even a youngster twelve years of age could understand and apply the techniques outlined herein.

All of the case histories presented in this book are of men and women who became rich by using the mental and spiritual laws described in it, and, to my personal knowledge, these people belong to all religious denominations. Moreover, they come from every income bracket and from every social level. All of these people have amassed wealth by thinking in a certain way, and by using the power of their subconscious mind in the right way.

The following are just some of the highlights of this book:

———How a salesman advanced from $5,000 to $50,000 annual income within a year.

————————How numerous people make use of a magic formula for paying bills with marvelous results.

————————How a business man in Los Angeles applied a million dollar formula, then moved from a "hole in the wall" to control a chain of stores worth many millions.

————————How a carpenter doing odd jobs became a skyscraper builder and amassed a vast fortune.

————————How a man who was broke, applied the specific three steps to riches, and then advanced by leaps and bounds along all lines.

————————The fascinating and thrilling story of how a wealthy miner conveyed the idea of riches to his son, who is now a famous surgeon, and the fact that his story supplies the key to riches.

————————How Mr. Tyng applied the age-old teachings of Truth and formed a multi-million dollar corporation. He took the formula for his riches from the Bible and proved that it works.

————————How poets, writers, artists, scientists, and business men draw riches from the treasure house of infinity within themselves.

————————How a boy ten years of age constantly receives gifts of money wherever he goes.

————————How to become rich in the knowledge of mental and spiritual laws, realizing that all the tangible good things of life thereafter will be added to you.

It is not possible for you to lead a full and happy life unless you are rich! There is a logical, scientific approach in becoming rich, and if you wish to reap the fruits of a rich, happy and successful life, you should study this book over and over again. Do exactly as it tells you to do, and you will open the way for yourself to grander, finer, happier, richer, and nobler living.

From this page onward, we shall venture together toward the riches of life here and now.

contents

9

The Magic Law of Tithing. (Continued)

A Grateful Heart Attracts Riches. (Continued)

Why give thanks?—The miracle of "thank you"—Value of gratitude—Do you appreciate your good?—The riches of forgiveness—Gratitude attracts fifty million dollars.

Using words with authority—His words brought him riches—How his word blesses— His word was made flesh—The living word works wonders—Words command the miracle power—How his words attracted clients—Her words settled an inheritance claim—Your healing words—His words caused them to pay—Her words opened a new door—Your words can solve your problems.

A genius in every man—How he drew wealth from the silence—His silent period made him famous—A thrilling experiment in the silence—How a mother recharged her batteries—How a pilot practices the silence— He solved his problem in the silence—How to get thrilling results—How to lead a charmed life—A scientist and the silence— Why nothing happened—The wise silence of Emerson—Begin to reap rich dividends daily—That inner stillness.

Your Infinite Power to Be Rich

chapter 1

The Treasure House of Infinity

THE Bible says, *I am come that they might have life, and that they might have it more abundantly. (John 10:10.)*

You are here to lead a full and happy life, to glorify God and enjoy Him forever. All the spiritual, mental, and material riches of the universe are the gifts of God, good in themselves and capable of a good use.

God is the giver and the gift; man is the receiver. God dwells in man, and this means that the treasure house of infinite riches is within you and all around you. By learning the laws of mind, you can extract from that infinite storehouse within you everything you need in order to live life gloriously, joyously, and abundantly.

Your Right to Be Rich

You were born to be rich. You grow rich by the use of your God-given faculties, by tuning in with the Infinite, and as your mind becomes productive and full of good ideas, your labor will become more productive and will bring you all kinds of material riches.

It is your feeling of oneness with God in your heart that makes you rich, and you are rich according to your mental attitude and faith in all things good. All of the riches of the Infinite—within and without—are yours to enjoy.

There is no virtue whatsoever in poverty, which in actual fact is a mental disease, and it should be abolished from the face of the earth. You are here to find your true place in life, and to give of your talents to the world. You are here to expand and unfold in a wonderful way, according to a God-given potential, and to bring forth spiritual, mental, and material riches which will bless humanity in countless ways. Learn how to surround yourself always with beauty and luxury, and realize your inalienable right to life, liberty, freedom, and peace of mind.

It is your Divine right to dramatize, reveal, portray, and express the power, elegance, and riches of the Infinite One.

The Science of Getting Rich

This is a universe of law and order, and there are principles and laws by which all of our experiences, conditions, and events take place. There is a definite law of cause and effect in everything. The science of getting rich is based on the law of belief. *If thou canst believe, all things are possible to him that believeth.* (*Mark 9:23*.) The law of life is the law of belief. To believe is to sincerely accept something as true. Believe in the abundant life, the happy life, the successful life, and live in the joyous expectancy of the best, and invariably the best will come to you. It is the belief of man that makes the difference between wealth and poverty, between success and failure, and between health and sickness. It is a cosmic law that *like thoughts always produce like effects;* therefore, any man who boldly claims the riches of the Infinite will receive them.

You Were Born to Be Rich

You were born with all the equipment necessary to lead a full, happy, and successful life. You were born to win, to conquer, to rise above all obstacles, and to demonstrate the glories and beauties within you. All the powers, qualities, attributes, and aspects of God are within you. Your life is God's life, and that life is your life now. God is always successful in whatever He undertakes, whether it is a tree or a cosmos. You are one with the Infinite, and you can't fail.

You are not here to earn a mere living. Life is a gift to you. You are here to express life and to give of your hidden talents and abilities through your mind, body, and soul. Your desires for health, abundance, happiness, peace, and true place in life represent the urges, promptings, and intimations of Infinite Life seeking expression through you. Desire now to make the most of yourself!

A Businessman's Three Steps to Riches

A business friend of mine in Beverly Hills said to me in his store, "My brother is in the same business as I am, just three blocks away, and he is prospering and rolling in wealth. Recently he hired two additional sales clerks. Yet, I can't make ends meet. It is not the environment or the merchandise; it must be me!"

I commented that getting rich and advancing in life is not a matter of a certain business or a certain location, that riches are of the mind of man, and that some men of great talent remain poverty-stricken and frustrated, while others who have very little talent or education prosper beyond their fondest dreams. I told him about three steps to unfailing riches.

He followed these three steps and progressed remarkably:

First Step: Never make a negative statement about finances, such as, "I can't pay the rent," "I can't make ends meet," "Business is very bad," "I can't pay my bills," etc. As soon as the negative thought, "I can't . . ." comes to mind, affirm instead: "I am one with the Infinite storehouse within me, and all my needs are met instantaneously." It may be necessary to do this fifty times in one hour, but persist and the negative thought will cease to trouble you.

Second Step: Make it a habit during the course of the day to condition your mind to the riches of the Infinite by affirming: "God is an ever present help in time of trouble," and, "God is the instant and immediate source of my supply, presenting me with all the ideas necessary at every moment of time and point of space."

Third Step: Lull yourself to sleep every night by reiterating this great truth: "I am ever grateful for God's riches that are ever active, ever present, unchanging, and eternal."

This businessman faithfully followed this spiritual prescription, and he has advanced by leaps and bounds. He framed the following Biblical quotation which stands on his desk: *The wilderness and the parched land shall be glad; and the desert shall rejoice, and blossom as the rose.* (*Isa. 35:1.*)

Recently, he said to me, "My mind was a wilderness and a desert. There was nothing growing there but weeds of ignorance, fear, self-depreciation, and a sense of unworthiness. Now I am on the way to victory, achievement, and prosperity."

Abundance of Opportunity

You are now in the space age, the age of superjets, electronics, space travel, and countless innovations and discoveries in the realms of science, art, medicine, and industry. For example, the fields of computers and electronics are still in their infancy and they offer endless scope for enterprise; and traffic through the air—even to other planets—undoubtedly becoming a vast industry, giving employment to countless thousands and perhaps millions of people all over the world.

There is abundance of opportunity for men and women who will go with the current of life and cease swimming against the tide. The law of riches is the same for you as it is for all others.

It has been said that the amount of fruit that falls to the ground and rots in the tropics every year would feed the whole world. Nature is lavish, extravagant, and bountiful. Man's shortage and lack comes because of his mal-distribution and abuse of nature's bounty. Look at the building materials here in the United States. There is enough timber, stone, cement, iron, steel, and other material to build a mansion for every living person in this country. There is enough material to clothe all women like queens, and all men like kings!

The visible supply, to all intents and purposes, is inexhaustible. You know that the Infinite Source is inexhaustible. It is the fountain that never runs dry. All things in this universe are made out of one universal, primordial substance. The only difference between copper, lead, gold, silver, wood, stones, or the watch on your wrist, is the number and rate of motion of the electrons revolving around a nucleus. The whole world and all things therein contained are made out of this universal primordial substance.

The Infinite storehouse of ideas within you never runs lean. If men need more gold and silver, they can make it synthetically from already-existing elements. Infinite Intelligence responds to your needs, and it is Its constant nature to enlarge Itself and to find a fuller expression through you.

She Found Riches Within Herself

A woman who listens every morning to my radio program wrote to me and said, "Bills are piling up; I am out of work. I have three children and no money. What shall I do?"

I suggested that she relax and condense the idea of her needs into a little phrase: "God supplies *all* my needs now." The significance of these words to her meant the realization of all her desires, such as bills paid, a new position, a home, a husband, food and clothing for the children, and an ample supply of money.

She repeated the phrase over and over again like a lullaby. Each time she affirmed, "God supplies all my needs now," a feeling of warmth and peace stole over her until she reached the point of conviction, and felt the reality of it.

This woman shortly achieved astonishing results! Her sister, whom she had not seen in fifteen years, visited her from Australia, and gave her $5,000 in cash as well as other gifts. She then became a secretary to a doctor, and married him within one month; she is now supremely happy. The ways of the Infinite truly are past finding out! This woman has truly found the storehouse of riches within herself.

Poverty Is a Disease

Disease means a lack of ease, poise, balance, and equilibrium. Look around you, and you will find people in all walks of life, and in all types of businesses and professions who are getting rich and achieving their goals in life, while others living near by them and in the same work and professions remain poor, ill-clad, and ill-fed.

If you were physically ill, you would visit your doctor and

have a physical checkup, in order to correct the condition at once. No matter how poor you may seem to be, if you habitually begin to think of riches, advancement, expansion, and progress, you will automatically receive a healing response from your subconscious mind, and your good fortune will be multiplied and magnified in countless measures and ways.

You may be in debt, however, and have no funds, influence, or tangible assets; but if you will begin to claim: "God's wealth is circulating in my life, and there always is a Divine surplus," wonders will soon happen in your life!

"It Was a Miracle!"

As I was writing this first chapter of this book, an elderly woman phoned me and said, "It was a miracle!" She and her husband had been receiving a very small pension and barely could make ends meet. I had given her a special prayer to use, as follows: "God's wealth is circulating in my life. His wealth flows to me in avalanches of abundance, and I give thanks for my good now and for all of God's riches."

She had kept repeating this prayer knowingly and feelingly many times during the day, and at the end of about two weeks, a man called at her door (she said he was "out of the blue") and asked her about a lot which she owned in the center of a desert. There were no homes there, no water—only brush and cactus. She had tried for years to sell it, and no one would even look at it. The man said, "Our company wants it to install electricity and power there for construction purposes nearby."

She was given $10,000 for the so-called worthless lot. This was not a miracle; it was the response of her subconscious mind[1] to her request. Its Infinite ways are past finding out.

[1] See *The Power of Your Subconscious Mind*, by Joseph Murphy. Published by Prentice-Hall, Inc., Englewood Cliffs, N.J., © 1963.

You Can Get Capital

Thought is the only intangible and invisible power of which you are aware. Whatever you think tends to manifest itself in your life, unless you neutralize it by a contrary thought. Your thought definitely and positively can produce for you tangible capital through your subconscious mind.

Your subconscious mind moves as it is acted upon by your thought. If you think "poverty" thoughts, you will become poor —no matter how rich you may now be. If you make a habit of thinking of riches, spiritual, mental, and material, you must become rich according to the law of reciprocal relationship. In other words, when you think, "Wealth is mine now," and remain faithful to that idea, your subconscious mind will respond by distributing to you wealth along all lines according to the nature of your thought life.

All inventions—buildings, structures, cities, and devices of all kinds, including all man-made forms and processes as well as those of nature—came out of the same type of invisible storehouse within you. When you think of moving from your chair, you make that motion. The scientist thought of projecting voices and harmonics into your home; television was the result. The electronic impulses were transmuted into form, voice, music, etc. You are really living in a "thought world."

The Infinite Presence thought of a world, and the Universal Mind moved according to that thought and took the form of a physical, dynamic universe, plus its system of stars, suns, and moons, and the endless galaxies in space. All this is the product of an Infinite Thinker, thinking in an orderly, mathematical manner and with absolute precision.

The poet Joyce Kilmer said, "Only God can make a tree." In creating the trees, whether oak or apple or what have you, the Infinite Thinker thinks of trees, and the Universal Mind starts in motion the forces bringing forth all trees according to their nature as prescribed by the principle of growth which is constant throughout Nature.

The Great Law of Attraction

Some months ago, a man showed me an invention of an engineering nature and said to me, "I need money to promote this—lots of money."

I explained to him that there is a law of attraction which would supply him with everything he needed for the fulfillment of his dream. I suggested that he make a practice of claiming mentally: "Infinite Intelligence within my subconscious mind attracts to me the ideal concern which will manufacture, promote, and sell this invention. There are mutual satisfaction, harmony, and Divine agreement which bless all concerned." This statement became his habitual prayer.

His subconscious got busy, and shortly thereafter he met a prominent business man in the Wilshire Ebell Theatre in Los Angeles where I was lecturing. This business man sponsored the invention and contracted with the proper parties to make the most of the invention. He has recently told me that it is going to be a fabulous product of a revolutionary nature, with unlimited profit potential.

This demonstrates the law of attraction, and, like the subjective wisdom of a seed which attracts to itself everything needed to enable its growth, man also can consciously draw forth the wisdom and ideas necessary for the fruition of his ideals, goals, and objectives for accumulating wealth.

Remember, all man-made forms, processes, and anything else he creates, must first live in man's thought-life; he cannot mold, fashion, or shape anything until he has thought it out. In the end, thought rules the world.

CHAPTER SUMMARY

Think and Gain Riches

1. Use the laws of mind and extract from the infinite storehouse within you everything you need to lead a glorious and successful life.

2. You were born to be rich, and you are here to lead a full and happy life. God wants you to be happy.

3. There is a definite law of cause and effect in everything. Believe in God's riches, and you shall receive. It is done unto you as you believe.

4. God always is successful in all His undertakings. You are one with God; therefore, you can't fail. You were born to conquer.

5. All riches are of the mind. It is your mental attitude that determines wealth or poverty. Think riches and riches follow; think poverty and poverty follows.

6. There is an abundance of opportunity for you. Go with the current of life and stop swimming against the tide. There is an infinite number of ideas to draw out of your subconscious; a new idea you have may be worth $50,000.

7. A magnificent way to contact the infinite storehouse within is to make a habit of affirming: "God supplies all my needs now." Wonders happen as you pray this way.

8. Poverty is a mental illness. Claim boldly, "God's wealth is circulating in my life and there is always a Divine surplus."

9. Your subconscious mind, which is the storehouse of riches, responds to your sincere thoughts in ways you know not of.

10. Thought is the only immaterial and invisible power of

which you are aware. Your thought definitely and positively can produce capital for you.

11. The law of attraction attracts to you everything you need, according to the nature of your thought life. Your environment and financial condition are the perfect reflection of your habitual thinking. Thought rules the world.

chapter 2

Riches
Are All Around You

T HE Bible says: . . . *The earth is full of the goodness of the Lord.* (*Ps. 33:5.*) Riches are all around you for the simple reason that the Divine Presence, though invisible, is omnipresent, or present everywhere.

It is like the air around us: there is no shortage of it. Each man can breathe in all he wants, and there is still an endless supply of air left. You may liken this Presence to the ocean. You may go to the ocean with a thimble and take a thimbleful of water, or you can go with a demijohn and fill it; the ocean doesn't care, and there is plenty of water left.

This Presence is infinite life; there is no life apart from it. This Presence also is infinite substance, in the same way that your thoughts and feelings are the substance behind everything you are, possess, and do.

Your conscious "at-one-ment" with this Presence overcomes all sense of deprivation or want because this Presence is fullness of being, the living fountain from which all blessings flow and which supplies everything that exists.

There is plenty of everything as well as an abundance of opportunity for the man who will tune in with the Infinite and think big. He will gain a response from the Presence and thereby bring all manner of good into expression in his immediate environment.

It is the Father's good pleasure to give you the kingdom of health, happiness, peace, joy, and abundance in material things.

There Is Enough of Everything

Begin now to clearly realize that the creative power within you is *unlimited;* then there is no reason whatsoever for limiting the extent to which you may enjoy and experience what you can create by means of this power. You are drawing from the Infinite Source, and you need never worry about taking more than your share because the infinite storehouse is inexhaustible and eternal, the same yesterday, today, and forever.

Man's great folly is in not realizing the true riches within himself and in looking upon external products, possessions, and conditions as being the true riches instead of the creative power of his own mind.

Remember, there is no limit in taking what you will from the infinite storehouse. Your true wealth consists in identifying yourself with the source of opulence and great riches. Think opulence, that is, think big, think generously and liberally, and you will find good flowing to you from all quarters, such as money and countless other things, all representing different facets of wealth.

Omnipotence is within you; therefore, there is plenty of power available to you. Infinite peace, boundless joy, and absolute harmony, plus an infinite number of ideas for success, expansion, improvement, and advancement and creativity along all lines are available in endless variety for the man who joins up with the infinite riches of God within him. "All things be ready, if the mind be so."

How He Implanted Riches in His Mind

I have a letter from a businessman, the substance of which states that he was brought up to believe that poverty was a virtue, and that he knew this superstitious belief implanted in his subconscious was blocking the improvement of his personal welfare and expansion in business. However, after listening to a series of my lectures on Sunday morning, he affirmed several times a day as follows:

"God's wisdom, power, and creative energies are extended and expressed through me, just as a branch of a tree is an extension of the life of the tree. I am a son of God, and I inherit all the rights, privileges, and blessings of God's riches. I center my mind on God and sense my oneness with this invisible Presence. I believe in infinite substance and infinite supply. I believe and mentally accept now that the Infinite is showering me with Its riches, bringing harmony, inspiration, blessings, and abundance into my life. I am one with my Father. His creative power is mine. His wisdom, strength, intelligence, and understanding are also my wisdom, strength, intelligence, and understanding. Infinite Intelligence directs me in all my ways, and His spirit of opulence is my abundance, success, and well-being. I open my mind and heart to the riches of the Infinite, and prosperity follows all my efforts. God and man are one. My Father and I are one."

The above prayer is very beautiful and also effective. This man continued to repeat these truths three or four times every day in his office. The result has been that he has opened three additional stores and has employed twenty-five more people to supervise and handle the business.

The so-called miracle was simply a redirection of his mind and a cultivation of the spirit of opulence.

The Cause of His Financial Trouble and Its Reversal

A young boy of about sixteen years of age in my neighborhood came to see me. He complained that his father would not allow him to go to college and become an engineer. His father was constantly saying, "We don't have the money to send you to college. We can't meet the mortgage on our home or the note that is due at the bank. We never make ends meet. Forget it!"

You can see the reason for this father's financial lack. He was constantly dwelling on lack, limitation, and financial restrictions of all kinds, and his subconscious naturally responded according to the nature of his habitual thinking. Think rich and riches follow; think poverty and poverty follows.

His Reversed Attitude Worked Wonders

I explained to this boy's father that all he needed was to cultivate the feeling of opulence and to constantly imagine that he possessed all kinds of riches. As a result, every night prior to sleep he imagined that he had received a letter from his son, telling him how happy he was to be in college and thanking him for all he had done for him. Furthermore, he claimed silently and feelingly: "God is the eternal source of my supply, meeting all my needs at every instant."

During the day when thoughts came to his mind, such as "I am short of money. I hardly know how to pay my bills. What have I to give? I am broke," etc., he never permitted the sentence to be finished in his mind. He persisted in neutralizing the negativity by immediately affirming: "God is the constant source of my supply, meeting all my needs instantaneously." Often, at first, he had to do this thirty or forty times in one hour, but after a few days the momentum and force of the habitual negative thoughts died out, and he ceased to be troubled by them.

Then, almost miraculously, he won a large sum of money from a lucky lottery ticket which paid all his debts and gave him increased confidence and faith in the power of his mind to meet all his needs at all times everywhere.

Today his son is in a university of his choice and is deeply grateful for the discovery of the real riches. This father and son will no longer tremble in fear and trepidation when financial exigencies and emergencies loom up before them.

Magic Formula for Paying Bills

A pharmacist in London, England, who attended my lectures some years ago, told me that he started his chemist's shop on a shoestring, so to speak. He opened his pharmacy on money borrowed from his father-in-law, who constantly pressed him for repayment. Bills were unpaid, and he was in desperate straits.

However, in one of the lectures at Caxton Hall in London some years previously, he had heard one of my statements: "Whenever you receive a bill for anything, immediately give thanks that you have *received* that same amount." After pondering this philosophy a bit, he began to do this regularly and systematically, and inasmuch as whatever the mind gives attention to magnifies and multiplies exceedingly, his business began to improve: three doctors in his neighborhood began to direct all their prescriptions to his pharmacy. I am happy to say that today he is the proud owner of three very successful pharmacies in the city of London.

The thought-image of receiving the amount of the bill gradually had sunk into his subconscious mind, and he knew the thought-image of the money was the substance of things hoped for and the evidence of things not seen. I have taught this magic formula to many businessmen, and in every case they are eternally grateful for its benefits. *And all things, whatsoever ye shall ask in prayer, believing, ye shall receive.* (*Matthew 21:22*)

How to Handle Financial Problems

The first principle in the art of becoming rich is to realize that thought is the only intangible power which can produce tangible riches from the storehouse of the Infinite.

Every created thing, every form and every process you see in this universe is the visible manifestation of a thought of Infinite Intelligence. As the Infinite thinks of a motion, the thought becomes that motion; as He thinks of a form, the thought takes on that form. This is the way all things were created in this world. You live in a thought world, and in order to become rich and to solve your financial problems you must continuously dwell on thoughts of wealth, prosperity, and success.

The Infinite had to think of a sequoia tree to bring it into being, and the thought proceeded to produce the tree even though centuries may have been required to bring it to completion. The Infinite Thinker, when It thought of a sequoia tree, did not cause the instant formation of a full-grown tree, but He started in motion all the forces necessary to produce the tree through the subjective wisdom operating in the seed.

Likewise, when you desire to be free from all financial problems and all sense of pecuniary embarrassment, you must realize that you are a thinker and that you can originate ideas, images, plans, and purposes. Furthermore, become aware that all structures, inventions, and all things fashioned by your hands first existed in your mind as thought-images. You cannot create anything in this world until you have *thought* that something into existence.

This being true, saturate your mind with these truths, such as: "I have absolute trust in God and all things good. I know that I will be able to meet any situation at any time, for God is my immediate source of supply, presenting me with all necessary ideas, in the right way and at the right time. God's riches are forever flowing freely in my life, and there is always a Divine surplus. As I repeat these truths, I know my mind is being conditioned to receive Divine supply forever flowing."

As you reiterate the above truths and feel the reality of them in your heart, you will develop the spirit of opulence, and regardless of the economic situation, stock market fluctuations, or other circumstances, you will always be amply supplied, no matter what form money power may take.

From $5,000 to $50,000 a Year

A few years ago a salesman who attends my Sunday lectures and who listens to my daily radio program asked me, "How can I make $50,000 a year? I am married and have three children. I barely make ends meet. My wife has to work in order for us to break even!"

In many instances, the explanation is the cure. I explained to him that the thought-image or mental pattern of wealth in his mind is the *first cause* relative to that thing; it is the actual substance of wealth, untouched by any previous conditions of lack, limitation, or restrictions of any kind.

His starting point was the thought-image. He realized that this is the modus operandi for all expression, whether on the scale of the Universal Mind, or his individual mind—which is itself a part of the Universal Mind. This salesman concluded that all he had to do was to communicate his thought-image to his subconscious mind and the result or manifestation of his idea would come forth.

The following is the sequel to our conversation, based on his letter to me:

"Dear Dr. Murphy: Shortly after I talked to you, every morning for the following three months I gave myself the mirror-treatment. I stood before my mirror after shaving and decreed out loud, slowly, feelingly and knowingly: 'John, you are a tremendous success. You are making $50,000 a year. You are an outstanding salesman.' I kept repeating this for about ten or twelve minutes every morning, knowing that finally I would build in my subconscious mind the mental equivalent of $50,000 and that I would succeed in psychologically impregnating myself with that amount. I was guided to take up public speaking; I gave a talk about ten weeks ago at our annual sales meeting. The vice president congratulated me, I was promoted, and I was given a more lucrative district at $10,000 annual salary. My commissions and salary the past year have exceeded $50,000! Truly the mind is the source of wealth and all the riches of Heaven."

He Worked Hard and Got Nowhere

One time I interviewed a junior executive who said, "I work very hard, spend long hours in the company, and I pray every night, saying, 'God is prospering me in all my ways, and I accept my good now.' Yet I get nowhere, and I have not had an increase in salary in five years or a promotion of any kind."

He admitted, however, that he was jealous and envious of the success and promotions of former classmates in the organization. His former college friends had gone up the ladder of success and excelled him; he was bitter and critical of their progress. *This was the reason he got nowhere.*

Thinking negatively of his associates and condemning their wealth, promotion, and success, caused the wealth and prosperity for which he was praying—to flee away and vanish. He was condemning the things he was praying for! He was hurting and injuring himself, because *he* was the one thinking and feeling these negative states of mind. Actually, he was praying two ways. On the one hand, he was saying, "God is prospering me now," and in the next breath, silently or audibly, he was saying, "I resent that fellow's promotion and increase in salary."

He began to realize that his mind is a creative medium, and the thoughts we think about another person, we bring to pass in our own experience. He reversed his mental attitude and made it a special point to wish for all his associates health, happiness, peace, and all the blessings of life. He made it a habit to rejoice in their prosperity, promotion, and success, and as he continued in this attitude, promotion and advancement came to him. His changed attitude changed everything.

A Sure Way to Become Financially Secure

Money is a medium of exchange. It is a symbol of freedom, beauty, luxury, power, refinement, and rich and joyous living. Money may be looked upon as a Divine idea, maintaining the economic health of the nations. It should be used wisely, judiciously, and constructively.

You become financially secure by impressing in your mind that money is not only good, but very good, and it blesses mankind in countless ways. In your mind, continue to imagine that you are a distribution center, that you possess all sorts of riches and that you are bestowing these blessings on others. As you do this, you are opening the way for still greater supplies to flow in.

Your motive is right, and you know in your heart that you have the right to plenty of money; you expect it to flow in avalanches of abundance. Your security and happiness are the results of the wise use of the power and wisdom resident in your subconscious mind.

Life will reward you when you believe and accept success as your Divine right. The real key to financial security is to constantly feel, know, and imagine yourself serving others in a grander, greater and more wonderful way. Imagine greater and greater success and abundance happening to you. Accept all monies received with a deep appreciation, and use it freely with grateful acknowledgment to the Infinite Being from whom all blessings flow.

Use the following prayer frequently, and you will convey the idea of financial security to your subconscious mind:

"I know that money is an idea in Divine Mind. It symbolizes wealth; I recognize it as a means of exchange. All of God's ideas are good. God created all things; He pronounced His creation good and very good. Money is good. I use it wisely, judiciously, and constructively. I use it to bless mankind. It is a very convenient symbol; I rejoice in its circulation. God's ideas are instantly available to me; I have a Divine surplus. God is my source of supply; that is my supply now. Wealth of all kinds flows to me in avalanches of abundance. There is only One God and One Mind; every idea in the Mind of God is spiritual. My relationship to money is friendly. It is a symbol of God's wealth and His infinite abundance. The idea of money is omnipresent; I am one with all of the wealth in the world. I use it for good only and I thank thee, Father, for thy supply."

CHAPTER SUMMARY

Highlights to Recall

1. Riches are all around you, for the simple reason that you live, move, and have your being in God; and God lives, moves, and has His being in you. God is omnipresent;

therefore, all of His riches are present everywhere, within you, and all around you.

2. The creative power in you is unlimited and inexhaustible. Your true wealth is in identifying yourself with the spirit of opulence.

3. Stay your mind on God and sense your oneness with the infinite storehouse of riches within, and riches will flow automatically into your life.

4. If you think of lack, limitation, and restrictions, you will create more lack and limitations of all kinds. What you give your attention to, you magnify in your world.

5. Realize that God is the eternal source of your supply meeting all your needs at every instant, and wonders will happen in your life.

6. A magic formula for paying bills and banishing all debts is to give thanks that you have received that amount of money when you receive any kind of a bill, and the idea will gradually impregnate your subconscious mind.

7. Your thought is the only immaterial power you know, and your thought can produce tangible riches from the invisible storehouse. Think riches and riches follow; think poverty and poverty follows.

8. Your thought-image or mental pattern of wealth is first cause relative to wealth. It is the substance of things hoped for and the evidence of things not seen.

9. To condemn the wealth and prosperity of another is to hurt yourself. Your mind is a creative medium, and what you wish for the other you are wishing for yourself. You are the thinker, and your thought is creative.

10. You will become financially secure by mentally identifying yourself with the eternal source of supply which never runs dry, and by having a deep desire to serve others in a grander, greater, and nobler way. God will supply all your needs and there will always be a Divine surplus.

chapter 3

Knowledge Is
Wealth

THE greatest discovery you can make is to be made aware that there is an infinite power and wisdom resident within you, enabling you to overcome all problems, to rise above all hurdles, and to handle life's tasks. You were born to conquer, and you are equipped with all the necessary attributes, qualities, and potentials to make you a master of your fate and a captain of your soul.

If you do not know of your spiritual powers, you will be governed and controlled by events and conditions of the world; you will tend to disparage yourself and generally to hold a low estimate of yourself. In other words, due to your lack of knowledge you will exalt the power of circumstances and fail to realize the tremendous powers within you, which could lift you up and set you on the high road to happiness, health, freedom, and the joy of living.

How Her Knowledge Paid Dividends

During a visit to the famous temple of Delphi near Athens, Greece, in August, 1965, I chatted with the guide. She was

fluent in English, French, and German, and her knowledge of
these languages had interested one of the tourists in our group,
who offered her a position as travelling companion in France
and Germany and also as governess of her three children in New
York City. The salary was to be $400 a month including living
quarters and food to be provided in the home. This guide told
me that her present salary was about 100 drachmas a day (a
little over $3.00). She said this opportunity was all like a big
dream, since she had wanted to go to the United States for many
years and now her wish was to be fulfilled.

The interesting thing about this young lady was that she had
been accustomed to praying fervently to the Blessed Virgin
every day for more money and for a trip to America; undoubtedly, her blind faith or belief had succeeded in impregnating
her subconscious mind, and definitely brought about this extraordinary response.[1] Paracelsus said: "Whether the object of your
faith be true or false, you will get the same results."

His Vision Was Wealth

I went on a lecture tour to England, Germany, Ireland, and
Greece, which included several days' vacation in each of the
countries visited. In Cork, Ireland, I had dinner in the home of
a young wine salesman and his charming wife. He was about
twenty-four years old. He told me that he had had a vision of
being the foremost wine salesman in the firm for which he worked
and that it recently had come to pass. He had been invited to the
headquarters in Dublin, and, at a formal ceremony, he had been
presented with an inscribed gold watch and a very large increase
in salary. He had been first in sales for three consecutive years.

Every night, this young man had affirmed prior to sleep: "I
am the foremost salesman, and I am handsomely compensated."

[1] See *The Power of Your Subconscious Mind*, by Joseph Murphy, published by Prentice-Hall, Inc., New Jersey, © 1963.

He would then mentally picture his wife congratulating him and go off to the deep of sleep. He is an avid reader of my book, *The Power of Your Subconscious Mind,* which has transformed his life.

This young man, who is a relative of mine, had no idea of competing with anyone. He has succeeded in impregnating his subconscious mind with the idea of "the foremost salesman," and his deeper mind—which always is responsive—had reacted in its own unique and extraordinary ways. Its Infinite ways are past finding out.

Knowledge Opens Doors

During my visit to the Temple of Apollo in Greece, I noticed a young Greek girl with a book under her arm. I thought that it looked familiar, and on closer observation I discovered to my astonishment that it was *The Miracle of Mind Dynamics.*[2] Immediately, I introduced myself, and she bombarded me with all kinds of interesting questions.

Her main problem was that she wanted to go to the United States, but she had been told at the U.S. Embassy in Athens that it would be years before she could expect to immigrate, due to the large waiting list. She said to me, "I have been using the techniques you have outlined in the book, and I have received answers to all my prayers but this particular one—permission to immigrate to the United States."

She had been affirming systematically, regularly, and faithfully: "Infinite Intelligence opens up the way for me to immigrate to the United States in Divine order. When man says, 'There is no way,' God says that there is, and I accept that way now."

I wrote a personal note for her to an extraordinarily brilliant woman attorney in New York, a student of Science of Mind and

[2] *The Miracle of Mind Dynamics,* by Joseph Murphy, published by Prentice-Hall, Inc., New Jersey, 1964.

an old friend of mine, explaining that this Greek girl had a
sister in business in New York for many years who was ill and
needed her sister in Greece to take care of the business and to
help her. The attorney acted almost immediately and wrote this
young student of *The Miracle of Mind Dynamics* in Greece and
told her what legal steps to take to insure her entry into the
United States.

As I wrote this very chapter I received a communication from
the young lady in Athens, who wrote: "It was no accident meeting you. When I saw you dressed in clericals and heard you
speak, I knew you were a minister from America. I also knew
that you would speak to me and that somehow you had the
answer for me."

I was simply the channel through which the infinite wisdom
of her subconscious had responded in answer to her constant and
persistent desire. She never faltered, vacillated, or questioned the
possibility of a way out of her dilemma. She simply knew that
there was an answer, and her persistence, stick-to-it-iveness, and
determination paid dividends.

The first step in the answer to her prayer happened when an
airline hostess presented her with a copy of *The Miracle of Mind
Dynamics,* saying: "This will help improve your English in a remarkable way, and if you use it, you will find yourself in
America."

The ways of the subconscious at times are entrancing, fascinating, enthralling, and captivating. You begin to realize that
wonders never cease and that "He never faileth."

Her New Concept Gained a Contract

In one of my lectures at Caxton Hall in London, England,
on this trip of which I have been writing, I spoke about *"The
Amazing Law of Love."*[3] After the lecture an actress chatted

with me and confided that she had quit the stage as she was bored to death with the scurrilities of the modern plays. "Now," she said, "I see where I have been at fault. I have something to give. I have been demoting myself and have been deeply resentful toward the publishers who committed mayhem on my new book. I am going out tomorrow and prove that love casts out fear, hate, and resentment."

I was in London just one week, and before I left this actress phoned me at my hotel on Bond Street and said proudly and joyously, "I signed a contract today! For two hours last night, I said aloud, 'Divine love fills my soul,' and I fell off to sleep with a deep feeling of love and goodwill to all mankind."

This actress had acquired a new idea of the meaning of love and had enthroned it in her mind, and she discovered that Divine love dissolves everything unlike itself. Love is the universal solvent. She had realized during the lecture that a base canard which was circulated about her and which particularly enraged her had no power to hurt her except through the medium of her own thought. She blessed those that had fabricated the absurd piece of gossip about her, and she was set free.

Today I Am Rich

I spoke to a small group in a private home in Munich, Germany, on the laws of mind. A young man, whose guest I was, is an outstanding Alpine ski teacher. On one of his excursions in Alpine climbing, one of his students—his fiancée—accidentally was lost in an avalanche and was found dead when discovered. He had been prosecuted by the law, and two courts found him guilty; at a third trial, however, he was exonerated from all cul-

---

[3] See *The Amazing Laws of Cosmic Mind Power,* by Joseph Murphy, published by Parker Publishing Company, Inc., West Nyack, © 1965.

pability. He had, nevertheless, a deep sense of guilt and suffered from acute remorse. Further, he felt hurt by denunciatory comments in the local press.

I explained to him that he could not be held responsible for the acts of others or for their wilful disobedience of instructions on alpine climbing. I also added that some people have a death wish and a death complex and they unconsciously choose some daredevil stunts which could result in their destruction. Self-loathing and self-hatred cause people to drink themselves to death, or to take an overdose of sleeping tablets or some other poison. He began to see that he was needlessly punishing himself and that, instead, he should bless the girl and release her to God, thereby freeing himself and his former fiancée.

I pointed out to him that all of us on this earthly plane come to pass, and that it is impossible to have one's mother, father, sister, brother, or loved one all the time. The time comes when each makes his or her transition. This is a cosmic law, and it is universal and applies to all men and women throughout the world. We must therefore listen to the murmurings and whisperings of our heart strings and realize that the passing on to the next dimension of each one of us is ordained by God and must be good or it would not be.

It is also wrong to hold morbid or depressed thoughts about loved ones[4] as this negative, depressed attitude holds them back. We must love them and release them to God, knowing that their journey is ever onward, upward, and Godward. When we think of them, let us realize that God's love fills their souls.

With this explanation, there was an effulgence of light in his eyes, and he exclaimed, "A load has been lifted from my mind! I am free. Today I am rich!"

[4] See "Every End Is a Beginning," page 63 of *The Miracle of Mind Dynamics,* by Joseph Murphy, Prentice-Hall, Inc., New Jersey, © 1964.

She Welcomed the Idea

During a visit to the Temple of Askleipios near Corinth, Greece, I listened with rapt attention as the guide explained how people in ancient times made pilgrimages to this ancient shrine and how they were healed of all manner of diseases. She dwelt on the fact that most of them were practically healed before they arrived because of their great expectancy, vivid imaginations, and blind belief. She added that ancient records reveal that the priests of the temple gave the sick ones drugs and put them into a deep hypnotic trance, and while in the trance state, the priest suggested to each one that the Goddess would visit him or her and a healing would follow. Archaeological research points out that undoubtedly many remarkable healings followed.

In discussing her lecture on the techniques employed in ancient times, I found she was thoroughly conversant with the workings of the subconscious mind and said, "Of course, Dr. Murphy, all the results which followed their sleeping at the shrine were due to the firm belief of those people that they would be cured of whatever infirmity they had, and according to their belief it was done unto them. Their fervent belief activated the healing current of their subconscious mind, which they attributed to various goddesses as well as to Askleipios, one of their ancient gods."

This young woman guide possessed riches of the mind. Her father was English and her mother Greek; she speaks both languages very well. She told me that she was born in one of the poorer neighborhoods of Athens, and that at times she could not go to school because her parents could not afford to buy her proper clothes. She prayed that God would give her the idea and tell her how to rise above the hypnosis of her condition, which was stifling all hope and causing acute mental depression.

The idea came to her spontaneously out of the blue, to teach American children the Greek language. Accordingly, she approached the wife of an executive of an oil company and offered her services. The woman said, "This is a wonderful idea!" and straightaway she engaged her at a handsome salary. Subsequently, this woman took her to the United States and other countries on a vacation, with all expenses paid.

Today the young woman is independently wealthy, but she still loves to tell tourists the history of ancient Greece, of its imposing temples, medieval castles, picturesque islands, and of the holy sanctuaries of ancient times. She did not treat lightly the idea which came to her. Instead, she acted upon it at once and proved to herself that ideas are our masters and that they hold sway over our fortunes in life.

Go all the way with your idea! Don't say, "Oh, that's too good to be true." Say, rather, "I welcome this idea! I accept it wholeheartedly and it will come to pass in God's good time."

Light Dispels Darkness

I had an interesting conversation with an Abbot of one of the famous Greek monasteries. He said that he felt the most powerful statement in the Bible is, *"He that is within you is greater than he that is in the world."* He added, "The realization that in the depths of my being there dwells God in His wisdom and power gives me confidence and assurance. When I ask for light or understanding on how to solve my problem, a new insight or idea wells up within me, and I see through the problem as the light of God dispels the darkness in my mind."

This Abbot has discovered the secret of life and the source of the riches of life. He said to me in parting, "Reality is not just what we see objectively in this phenomenalistic world, but also what we think, feel, imagine, and believe."

All he said, really, was what all students of the mind know, which is that Infinite Causation is *within* us, and not outside of us. Remember, the Creator is greater than His creation. The thinker is greater than his thoughts; the artist is greater than his art. Do not give power to sticks and stones or to external things. Give power, devotion, loyalty, and faith to the only creative power, which is in your thought and feeling. Your thought and feeling control your destiny. Your thought-image felt as true is *. . . the substance of things hoped for, the evidence of things not seen. (Hebrews 11:1)*

CHAPTER SUMMARY

Points to Recall

1. You are spiritually equipped to overcome and to triumph over all problems, hurdles, and difficulties in life.

2. Knowledge can pay you fabulous dividends. For example, knowledge of a foreign language can open up the way for wealth, travel, and exciting adventures along all lines.

3. Your vision or mental estimate of yourself activates your subconscious mind and compels you to be all that you imagine yourself to be. The law of your subconscious is compulsion.

4. Knowledge opens up closed doors. When man says, "There is no way," the Infinite wisdom within you says, *. . . I have set before thee an open door, and no man can shut it . . . (Rev. 3:8)* Trust this inner guide, and wonders will happen as you pray.

5. Get a bright new estimate of yourself. Your new concept will gain you new contacts, promotion, and untold wealth.

6. You are not responsible for the actions of another. All you owe the other person is love and goodwill. This frees you and absolves you from all sense of guilt.

7. Welcome the new idea which comes into your mind in response to your prayer. Go all the way with your idea. Come to a definite conclusion and prove to yourself that your new idea can bring riches into your life.

8. When stymied, blocked, or in a mental dilemma, get a new awareness, which means new light or understanding. Know that *He that is within you is greater than he that is in the world*. Believe this, and a new insight will be given you, enabling you to see through all problems. Remember that Light (understanding, fresh insight, truth, a new idea) dispels all darkness. Let the Infinite Light shine in you and all shadows of financial lack will flee away from you.

chapter 4

Get In Partnership
with God

IN my recent travels to the many beautiful islands of Greece, I met many tourists from Australia, Rhodesia, Union of South Africa, and other lands, and was amazed at the knowledge of the laws of mind possessed by many of these business and professional men. The consensus was that they aligned themselves with their Higher Self, and, as some of them said:

"We took God as our senior partner, and we asked for guidance in our work. We prayed that we would attract the right men to do the job and that Infinite Intelligence would reveal the perfect plan for the manufacture, sale, and distribution of our products. We attribute our success and achievements to the direction given us by our Higher Self."

Some of these men were builders, architects, engineers, business executives, and directors of mines and other vast holdings. They used God as their guide, advisor, and counsellor in all phases of their lives, *and they prospered beyond their fondest dreams.*

Many people put God into some sort of a pigeon hole to be

brought out only on holidays, at weddings, funerals, and other special occasions. God is not a being living up in the skies, but rather He is the wisdom and power which created you, started your heartbeat, grows hair on your head, and controls all your vital organs even when you are sound asleep. If you fail to recognize and use the wisdom and power within you, it is just the same as if it were not there.

God is the name for the infinite mind and intelligence within you. Actually, you are always using this power whether you know it or not. For instance, when you lift your finger, it is the power of God in you enabling you to do this. When you solve a problem, it is the creative intelligence within you revealing the answer. When you cut your finger the infinite healing presence proceeds to form a clot and to build new cells around it in order to restore it to wholeness. When you pour out love on your child you are using a part of the infinite love of God. When you are generating peace and poise, you are manifesting a part of the absolute peace of God. Join up with God, and let financial good happen in your life.

A Fortune to Share

At the island of Moni near Athens, I had a long talk with a writer from Johannesburg, South Africa. He brought out some interesting points, saying that many of his articles were regularly rejected, and that his first book was returned marked "not read" and "not interested." He was getting a rejection complex until he read a book dealing with the laws of mind, which transformed his thinking processes.

He then began to use his imagination more constructively. He would think about the characters in his novel, the particular situations, the plot, and about the truths he wished to expound, and then he would affirm boldly morning and night for about a half hour: "God's wisdom writes this novel through me. My intellect is illuminated, and I write a novel which inspires, blesses, and is a boon to mankind."

"Often," he said, "I wake up in the morning, and I find the novel writing itself through me; my conscious mind carries out the dictates from within."

All his writings have been accepted since he started this procedure. He found the rich storehouse within him and used it to elevate and to dignify the soul of man through his pen.

He discovered that his mind is a part of the one universal mind of God, and that when he used his mind in the right way he gained a response from his deeper mind. This writer attributes much of his financial success to his deep belief in the Biblical verse: *If any of you lack wisdom, let him ask of God, that giveth to all men liberally, and upbraideth not; and it shall be given him. (James 1:5.)*

Confidence Is Wealth

A crowning feature of a visit to Greece is a trip to Cape Sounion which is dominated by the spectacular white marble of the Temple of Poseidon, the God of the ocean. Sunset watched from this headland is a sight of rare splendor and indescribable beauty.

It was in this atmosphere that I conversed at length with my guide, and she told me her story. She was born in the poorest area of Athens and had a deep inferiority complex. As a girl, she used to watch tourists hire guides to drive them to the fabulous historic places in Greece. She said to her father and mother one day that she wanted to be smart and intelligent so that she could act as a guide, and they ridiculed her, reminding her that education was for the rich and that she was born on the wrong side of the street.

However, she clung to her idea, and as she grew up and went to high school she asked the principal if she could be an archaeologist. He said to her, "Yes, if you have confidence in yourself. And you get confidence by believing that 'God and I can do it.'"

She said to me, "I lived with that phrase in my heart, and I am now in my third year in archaeology and will be qualified in about two more years."

Her confidence in her power to become what she wanted to be was transformed into *money, enthusiasm, love of work, vitality, charm, and a wonderful, radiant personality.* This is her favorite Biblical quotation: *Finally, my brethren, be strong in the Lord, and in the power of his might. (Ephesians 6:10.)*

The idea of becoming an archaeologist was enthroned in her mind and became regnant and sovereign; then her subconscious mind, full of wisdom and power, brought it to pass in Divine order.

The Genius Is Within You

I had dinner with a prominent businessman from Capetown, South Africa, whom I met on this European tour. He said frankly that years ago he had failed four times in business ventures in Capetown, due primarily to listening to the advice of the so-called experts on where to open up business sites, how to buy, and how to promote and advertise. He added that the cause of all his trouble was that he had been leaning on others for advice, and that his misery, suffering, and failures were due to his lack of awareness of the genius within himself.

His wife suggested to him that he place his trust in his Higher Self. She typed a quotation from the Bible and advised him to live mentally with it, and then success would be assured him. This key to success was: *But my God shall supply all your need according to his riches in glory . . . (Phil. 4:19.)*

He thereupon began to tune in with the Infinite, realizing that every problem he met was Divinely outmatched because God—the All-Wise One—was within him and was responsive to his call. No longer did he look at conditions, circumstances, and problems as being greater than he; on the contrary, he knew that they could be solved and overcome. He began to tackle every difficulty with faith and confidence, knowing that there was a way out and that there was an exhilarating joy in overcoming them. He began to like the challenges he met on his way!

He discovered a wisdom and intelligence within him and ceased being a hypnotized victim of the conditions and circumstances which confronted him. Today he is a tremendous success and employs hundreds of people; and with the pleasure that comes from success, he is contributing to various institutions of higher learning and to charitable organizations. *Thou wilt keep him in perfect peace, whose mind is stayed on thee: because he trusteth in thee. (Isaiah 26:3.)*

You Can Triumph

I met a young doctor in the hotel where I stayed in Frankfurt, Germany, who told me that he had worked his way through college, paying all his expenses. When he graduated the thoughts came to him, "You have no money. You can't open in a nice neighborhood. You can't properly equip your office."

Having studied medical psychology, he knew that these were negative suggestions working on his mind and that, as such, they had no power whatsoever. He knew that the only creative power was his own thought and feeling. He placed his confidence on the creative power of his own mind, rather than on the false and limiting suggestions of circumstances.

He cleansed his mind of beliefs in impediments, obstructions, delays, and obstacles, and called on the creative power of his mind to open up the ideal office for him. He consistently and purposefully pictured himself in a sumptuous office, surrounded by all the latest accoutrements of his profession, and claimed that the infinite intelligence of his subconscious mind was now acting on his request, bringing it to pass in Divine order.

Shortly afterward, a woman called at his residence where he had set up a temporary office in his father's home. She was suffering from acute pain which he immediately diagnosed as acute appendicitis. He rushed her to the hospital, operated on her, and she had a remarkable recovery.

Eventually they fell in love. She not only financed a new office for him, but bought him a Rolls Royce which was delivered from England on their wedding day. His bride's father was an immensely wealthy industrialist, and he was delighted to have the opportunity of providing his son-in-law with all the modern equipment in this new age of medicine.

This shows you that you are not a victim of circumstances, except you believe you are. Allow the boundless wisdom of the Infinite One to flow through you, and all the financial conditions of your life will change—miraculously and immediately!

What you really need, like this young doctor, is to discover and become acquainted with your inner power, which is called self-realization. The God-man indwells you. Yet millions of people all over the world remain sick, frustrated, defeated, and poverty-stricken for the simple reason that they are wholly unaware of the God-Self within them.

Your job and my job is to become aware of this Divine Presence and to free ourselves from inhibitions, frustrations, and poverty. *Acquaint now thyself with him, and be at peace: thereby good shall come unto thee. (Job 22:21.)* Get acquainted with your inner powers, and you will experience happiness, prosperity, and peace of mind.

You can be just as happy on Hollywood Boulevard as living near the lakes of Killarney. In truth, location has nothing to do with your health, wealth, or success. You create your own success, wealth, and prosperity.

Your Higher Self is this moment speaking through you, urging you to move forward, upward, and God-ward. God speaks to each one of us through our desires, which in reality is the voice of God seeking expression through us.

You are the infinite keyboard of God, and you are here to play the melody of God. Begin your new assignment, job, study, be it what it may, with zest, enthusiasm, and confidence. In the mood with which you start, you will find yourself finishing on the same joyous note or tone. Begin with love of God, and you will finish loving the good or God. Begin your new job with a faith and a confidence in God, and you will be led to victory, triumph, and glory,—and certainly to financial success.

She Said the Beginning and the End Are One

I listened to a young musician play the harp in Killarney, Ireland. I was accompanied by a sister of mine who lives in England and who teaches French, Latin, and mathematics. My sister commented, "This is the most beautiful music I have ever heard. As a harpist, she is superb!"

We invited the young lady to our table for dinner, and she said, "Before I play I always pray this way: 'God, the Great Musician, plays through me. I am His servant, and I play for Him and He plays through me His own song, the melody of love, for God is love.' This is the way I begin, and the law of life is that the beginning and the end are one. I begin with love, praise, and adoration of things Divine, and the result must be the image and likeness of His love, His beauty, and His glory."

CHAPTER SUMMARY

Points of Interest

1. Get into partnership with God and you will grow rich.
2. You have a fortune to share. Find out the tremendous powei and wisdom resident in your subconscious mind, and you can become inspired, blessed, and prospered in countless ways. You can become a great boon to mankind.
3. Remember that your confidence, faith, and understanding of the laws of mind are translated into health, wealth, and success.
4. The genius is within you. When you are in tune and *en rapport* with the wisdom and intelligence of your subconscious, the genius in you will be revealed. The infinite intelligence in your subconscious mind can solve all your problems of financial supply and give you the right answers.
5. Every problem is Divinely outmatched. Conditions and circumstances are not creative; the creative power is in your thought and feeling rather than in the false and limiting suggestions of externalities.
6. The law of life is that the beginning and the end are one. Begin your new project with zeal, enthusiasm, faith, and confidence, and the result of your endeavors will be the image and likeness of the mood and tone in which you started. Begin with faith in the God-power within you, and you will have wonderful results in all your undertakings. including the financial ones.

chapter 5

How to Pray
and Grow Rich

IN the depths of the earth you may find countless riches, such as gold, silver, platinum, uranium, gas, oil, diamonds, and innumerable other precious stones and metals, plus the countless by-products arising from them. However, as previously pointed out, the real riches of life lie within the subliminal depths of man. It is the innate intelligence possessed by man that enables him always to find, to employ, and to distribute the treasures of the earth.

The most precious things in all the world are within you. For example, in your unconscious depths you will find boundless wisdom, infinite intelligence, limitless power, and all the wonders and glories of the God-Presence. You can ask for direction and guidance—and receive it. You can mine your inner riches and bring forth precious stones and jewels in the form of new creative ideas, inventions, discoveries, glorious music, new songs, and answers to all problems. Having found the storehouse of wealth within, you positively, definitely, and absolutely will find the external riches of nature. For, "as within, so without."

How She Discovered Spiritual Gold

Recently I received a letter from a woman, saying: "My husband and I have been married for thirty years. He is 65 and I am

51. We have been blessed with five children. We have had a happy, peaceful life—or so I imagined. Recently, however, my husband confessed to me that he had been having an affair for more than three years with a young stenographer in the office where he works. He has asked me in a cold-blooded manner to understand until the affair 'is all over with.'

"I am angry, hateful, resentful, and deeply hurt; the children are shocked. I am losing faith in myself, even though others say I am attractive, intelligent, and charming. I am brooding and can't sleep. I have been betrayed. I am in despair. What shall I do?"

I responded by explaining to her that her husband was undoubtedly morally weak and had a deep sense of inadequacy and inferiority. His dalliance with this protracted affair shows his loyalty and character have broken down, because he is exploiting this young woman, who is his co-worker, and for whom he feels no obligation or responsibility as is evident by his statement, "until it is all over with."

I included the following in my letter: "Your husband has a deep sense of guilt plus a great fear of consequences. He knows the devastating effects on you of telling you of the affair. Presumably the reason for this is that the young woman, i.e., his paramour, is putting the pressure on him to divorce you and to marry her.

"He is now in a 'double-minded state,' and while addicted to habitual connivance with his paramour, unconsciously he wants to remain united with you. Talk to your husband frankly and tell him point blank that he must have the moral courage, the mental discipline, and the essential manhood to break off the affair at once. Say that it must be done, as you will not continue to live this way because when there is no loyalty to one another in marriage, the latter becomes a farce, a masquerade, and a sham. His disclosure to you is possibly a desire on his part to line up with you before his paramour tells you about it and asks you to give him up."

I emphasized that she have the frank talk with her husband as pointed out above and also urged her to pray frequently as follows: "I radiate love, peace, goodwill, and joy to my husband. There are harmony, peace, and Divine understanding between us. I salute the Divinity in my husband, and Divine love unites us at all times. God thinks, speaks, and acts through him, just as He thinks, speaks, and acts through me. Our marriage is consecrated to God and His love."

She prayed in the above manner for about a week and then had a heart-to-heart talk with her husband. He thereupon wept copiously and begged her forgiveness. Today, harmony, peace, and love fill their home. Once this woman had decided to dig she shortly found the spiritual gold within herself.

The Gold Mine Within You

I recently had a most interesting conversation with a surgeon in Killarney, Ireland. He and his charming wife were touring the country. We began to talk about the wonders of the mind, and he told me a fabulous story about his father. This is the essence of it, and I am going to present it in the simplest possible way.

This young surgeon was the son of a miner in Wales. His father had worked long hours at very low wages; as a boy, the surgeon had had to go to school barefoot as his father could not afford to buy shoes for him. Fruit and meat appeared on the table twice a year, mainly at Easter and at Christmas; buttermilk, potatoes, and tea represented the main or staple diet of this family.

One day, this young man said to his father, "Dad, I want to be a surgeon, and I'll tell you why. The boy I am going to school with had cataracts; the eye surgeon operated on him, and now he sees perfectly. I want to do good like that doctor."

His father replied, "Son, I have set aside 3,000 pounds (about $8,000) which I have saved over a period of twenty-five years. It is set aside for your education, but I would rather you not touch it until such time as you have finished your medical education. You then can use it to open up a beautiful office in Harley Street (London area of specialists) with all the accoutrements of your profession. In the meantime, the money will be drawing interest, and you will have security. You know that any time you really need it during your medical studies you can always draw upon it. It is all yours, but I would prefer that you let it accumulate interest, and on your graduation it will be a nice 'nest egg' for you."

This thrilled the young man beyond words, and he vowed never to touch the money until he graduated from medical school. He worked his way through medical school, working in pharmacies at night and during holidays; he also earned money as an instructor in pharmacology and chemistry in the medical college. His whole idea was to live up to his promise to his father that he would not touch the money in the bank until he graduated.

The day came when he graduated, and his father told him, "Son, I have been digging for coal all my life and have gotten nowhere. There is not a shilling or a penny in the bank and there never was. I wanted you to dig deeply and find the treasures in the gold mine within yourself, which is limitless, inexhaustible, and eternal."

"For a moment," the surgeon said, "I was flabbergasted, dumbfounded, and inarticulate. After a few minutes, I got over the consternation and the shock, and then both of us burst out laughing. Then I realized that what Dad had really wanted to teach me was the feeling of wealth engendered by the thought of plenty of money in the bank to back me up if I needed it. It gave me courage, faith, and confidence and made me believe in myself. My belief that I had 3,000 pounds in the bank had accomplished the purpose just as well as if it actually had been deposited in the bank in my name."

This surgeon remarked that all that he had accomplished externally was but a symbol of his inner faith, vision, and conviction. There had been no money from the father to back up this medical student, not even a farthing, but look at the wonders it wrought in his life! For every man in the world, the secret of success, accomplishment, achievement, and fulfillment of his goal in life lies in the discovery of the miraculous power of his thought and feeling. Our surgeon friend *acted confidently*—just as if the money was always there!

His Investment Multiplied Exceedingly

Recently I received a letter from a man who attended a lecture I gave on "Your Subconscious Is a Bank." I quote in part:

"Dear Dr. Murphy, I listened to your lecture on using the subconscious mind as a bank. I had never looked at it that way before, but suddenly I realized that my thoughts, mental pictures, moods, and attitudes are investments in the subconscious. I became aware that I have been a sloppy thinker as I had been depositing in my subconscious mind, resentment, laziness, procrastination, fretfulness, and self-condemnation. It is true that my subconscious mind multiplied all these negatives exceedingly, and I ended up in the hospital with ulcers."

"It has been three months since I heard your lecture. The first night after hearing you, I began to think about God not as a man presiding in the heavens with the capriciousness and frailties of man, but as an Infinite Intelligence permeating all things and directing the entire cosmos and instantly responding to me. *I* began to claim out loud feelingly and knowingly: 'God's power, strength, peace, wisdom, and joy are mine now. His love fills my soul, and His light reveals to me better ways to serve mankind.'

"Since I began depositing these ideas in my personal bank (my subconscious mind), marvelous creative ideas have come to me from the gold mine within. My business has increased 300 percent. I am healthy, happy, joyous, and full of the laughter of God. It is wonderful!"

You Are Rich Now!

Relax, let go, and say to yourself, "I am going to dig mentally within myself and draw out some marvelous ideas for better service and accomplishment. I know that I have inner resources, powers, qualities, and abilities which I have never tapped. I know that Infinite Intelligence reveals them to me now as I consciously dig down into the storehouse within me."

You will be amazed how the new ideas which come to you can be turned into wealth. Recognize your inner treasure house, organize your ideas, and put them into action.

Your Idea Can Be Worth Billions

Coal lay in ledges under the ground since the days of the flood; a laborer seeking wealth used his pick to bring it to the surface. This discovery resulted in employment for millions of people all over the world and served as the means of amassing countless fortunes. Coal carries the heat of the tropics to the Arctic Circle and makes homes in the polar area as warm as those in Los Angeles.

A young Scotch boy, digging mentally within himself for a new idea which would make money for himself and for others, envisioned a fortune in the steam escaping from a tea kettle as it forced off the lid. All of a sudden the expansive force of the steam came to his mind, and this idea was the actual beginning of the steam engine which has revolutionized the world, has supplied work for untold millions, and thereby has caused the creation of fabulous wealth all over the world.

Someone recently brought to my attention a statement by Henry Ford. When he was asked what he would do if he lost all his money and his business, he replied, "I would think of some other fundamental, basic need of all people, and I would supply that need more cheaply and more efficiently than anyone else. In five years I would again be a multimillionaire."

Tremendous opportunities await you in this electronic and space age. Ask your deeper mind to give you new creative, inspirational ideas, and you will release the creative powers of your subconscious. You will find a need of humanity which in time will enrich and bless you. Begin now to release that imprisoned splendor within you!

Your Fortune Begins with You

Wealth and poverty have their origins in your own mind. You must come to a clear-cut decision that you intend to be wealthy and successful. Wealth is not a matter of chance, luck, or coincidence. *The only chance you have is the chance you make for yourself.*

A brilliant young executive said to me, "I work very hard and put in long hours. My suggestions and recommendations to the management have been accepted and have made money for the organization. But I have been passed up for promotion the past three years. Even my subordinates have received increments and promotion."

This man was industrious and intelligent and apparently worked arduously. The answer was in his relationship to his ex-wife.

For three years there had been litigation over division of their property, alimony, and child support. Subconsciously, he did not want to make any more money until the lawsuit was over as he felt the more money he made, the more alimony would be assessed by the court. He resented paying the temporary allowance granted by the court, feeling it was excessive, and he was waiting for final adjudication.

I explained to him the way his subconscious mind works and that actually he was decreeing that he didn't want any more money and had definitely emotionalized that negative concept. Furthermore, his resentment, hostility, antagonism, and wish to withhold wealth from his ex-wife was being impressed in his own subconscious mind and was being manifested in all phases of his financial life.

When you mentally wish to withhold wealth from another, you also automatically withhold it from yourself. This is why the golden rule tells you to think, speak, and act well toward your neighbor; and never to indulge in hate, resentment, or carping criticism for the simple reason that you are the only thinker in *your* universe, and your negative thoughts set up negative reactions in all departments of your life. Your subconscious mind is always fabricating and projecting on the screen of space the *totality* of your stream of thought-life.

This young executive perceived that he had been blocking his own expansion and promotion. The answer to his problem was within himself. He came to the stabilizing point within himself where he realized that love casts out hate and that as he wished health, love, peace, and prosperity to his ex-wife and his children, he would attract to himself equally all these qualities. He also began to see that she was entitled to a reasonable sum of money for the support of his three children, that he should give it gladly, joyously, and lovingly, and that as he gave freely it would return multiplied. He applied the following prayer frequently:

"God is love, and God is life. This life is one and indivisible. Life manifests itself in and through all people; it is at the center of my own being. I know that light dispels the darkness; so does the love of the good overcome all evil. My knowledge of the power of love overcomes all negative conditions now. Love and hate cannot dwell together. I now turn the light of God upon all fear or anxious thoughts in my mind, and they flee away. The dawn (light of truth) appears, and the shadows (fear and doubt) flee away.

"I know Divine love watches over me, guides me, and makes clear the path for me. I am expanding into the Divine. I am now expressing God in all my thoughts, words, and actions; the nature of God is love. I know that *perfect love casteth out fear.*"

In a few weeks' time, an inner transformation took place in this young man, and he became amiable, affable, genial, and loving. He had a spiritual rebirth. His financial affairs immediately took a turn for the better, and he received a handsome promotion.

The outcome was quite revealing. His ex-wife asked for a reconciliation, and the lamp of love which united them in the first place led them back to the altar where again their two hearts became one. . . . *What therefore God hath joined together, let not man put asunder. (Matthew 19:6.)*

How to Pray and Grow Rich

Here is a never-failing daily prayer for financial supply:

"I know that my good exists this very moment. I believe in my heart that I can prophesy for myself harmony, health, peace, and joy. I enthrone the concept of peace, success, and prosperity in my mind now. I know and believe these thoughts (seeds) will grow and manifest themselves in my experience. I am the gardener; as I sow, so shall I reap. I sow God-like thoughts (seeds);

these wonderful seeds are peace, success, harmony, and goodwill. It is a wonderful harvest.

"From this moment forward I am depositing in my subconscious mind seeds or thoughts of peace, confidence, poise, prosperity and balance. I am drawing out the fruits of the wonderful seeds I am depositing. I believe and accept the fact that my desire is a seed deposited in the subconscious. I make it real by feeling the reality of it. I accept the reality of my desire in the same manner as I accept the fact that a seed deposited in the ground will grow. I know it grows in the darkness; my desire or ideal grows in the darkness of my subconscious mind. In a little while, like the seed, it comes above the ground (becomes objectified) as a condition, circumstance, or event. This is the true source of my full financial supply.

"Infinite Intelligence governs and guides me in all ways. I meditate on whatsoever things are true, honest, just, lovely, and of good report. I think on these things, and God's power is with my thoughts of good. I am at peace, because I am infinitely prosperous."

Finally, brethren, whatsoever things are pure, whatsoever things are lovely, whatsoever things are of good report; if there be any virtue, and if there be any praise, think on these things. (Philippians 4:8.)

CHAPTER SUMMARY

Pointers in Review

1. The real riches of life lie in your subconscious depths. The treasure house is within you, and from it you can extract fabulous riches through objective prayer.

2. The smart wife does not give power to the mistress or para-

mour of her husband. She knows that he is mentally sick
and that the other woman is frustrated, neurotic, and in-
hibited. She frankly discusses the matter with her husband,
and she prays her way through it.

3. Riches are of the mind. Faith, confidence, zeal, enthusiasm,
   and a belief in yourself are translated into health, success,
   wealth, and accomplishment. A poverty-stricken boy became a famous surgeon by believing his father had plenty
   of money to pay all his expenses in medical school; yet the
   father did not have a penny to help him. Look at the magic
   wrought by the belief in the mind of the boy! Get acquainted
   with the nuances of your thought and feeling and transform
   your life!

4. Your thoughts, mental imagery, beliefs, attitudes, and feelings are investments which you deposit in your subconscious
   mind. Your subconscious gives compound interest, i.e., it
   magnifies whatever you deposit. Impress your subconscious
   with love, faith, confidence, right action, guidance, abundance, security, and good humor, and whenever you need
   love, confidence, or an answer to a problem, your subconscious will supply you. This is the way to dig treasures out
   of the gold mine within you.

5. The only chance you have is the chance you make for yourself. If you resent the wealth of another or if you mentally
   wish to withhold good from him, you not only are hurting
   yourself, but you are depriving yourself of the riches of life.
   You are the only thinker in your universe, and what you
   think you create. Create wealth by wishing for all men all the
   riches of heaven.

chapter 6

The Magic Law
of Tithing

THE word *tithe* means *one-tenth,* the proportion of man's income which has been devoted to sacred purposes from time immemorial. From the earliest times, tithes for the year's yield from fields, fruits, and flocks were offered to the service of God by peoples in lands from Babylonia to Rome.

The lack of uniformity in the Bible concerning the law of tithing is primarily due to the fact that the general principle of giving was practiced in different ways in different eras, and it was subject to regulations which changed under ecclesiastical and political pressures.

Tithing is one of the fundamental laws of life, and its practice is lost in antiquity. The farmer has to tithe in order to reap a harvest. His tithe is one-tenth of the grain, corn, barley, or oats which he gives back to the soil; otherwise, he would have no crop.

The ideal way to tithe your wealth is to give a certain percentage of your money, land, stocks, bonds, or any other form of material wealth, for the propagation of the Truth, usually in support of those churches or activities which are engaged in dissemination of the eternal verities of God.

The Real Meaning of Tithing

The tithes are not only the monies which you freely give to support the propagation of the truth of being and the spiritual activity of your choice, tithes also refer to your beliefs, convictions, estimates, and blueprints that you mentally accept as true about yourself, others, and the world in general. Whatever you consciously accept and believe as true about yourself, about God, and about the universe also constitutes the definite payments (impressions) given to the treasure house of your own subconscious mind.

Remember that Infinite Intelligence (God) responds to the nature of your thought. God will do nothing for you except through your own thought, imagery, and belief. God has created you and He has established the universe and all things therein contained. You are here to draw forth the power and wisdom within you and to lead a full, happy, and prosperous life. You are also here to contribute to the riches, prosperity, success, and the good of others.

A Lawyer Discovers the Magic of Tithing

I explained to a lawyer friend of mine, who had told me of one of his problems, the spiritual meaning of tithing. This lawyer was required to go to New Orleans on behalf of a client. This client had explained to him that an attorney in Louisiana, with whom he was about to visit, was nasty, obstreperous, belligerent, and most uncooperative.

I suggested to the lawyer that he tithe, i.e., assume that the action of God would take place in the mind and heart of the attorney in question and that his mental judgment or conviction should be such that there would be a harmonious and Divine solution, blessing all concerned.

As a result, prior to his visit, my lawyer friend prayed frequently that harmony, peace, love, and understanding would reign supreme at his conference with the other attorney in New Orleans. When the conference finally took place, the utmost cooperation, cordiality, and geniality actually governed the meeting. This resulted in a satisfactory legal and financial settlement for all concerned.

Action and reaction are universal and constant. Your thought is action. Reaction is the response of your subconscious mind according to the nature of your thought.

The most significant point to realize is that the spiritual idea (tithe) in back of any interview, transaction, or activity is the reality of it. The above-mentioned attorney quickly realized the profound truth that everything you do takes its tone and color from your assumption and belief regarding it.

The Law of Tithing Works Wonders for Sales Manager

A prominent sales manager who attends my lectures once told me that he tithes prior to giving a sales talk to his two hundred salesmen. If he speaks for an hour, he gives one-tenth of that hour to God. There are sixty minutes in an hour, and he regularly devotes six minutes to prayer and meditation prior to his lectures to the sales force. He tithes as follows:

"I am filled with the wisdom, love, and power of God. All my salesmen are guided, directed, inspired, and receptive to new ideas. I am inspired and illuminated from On High in my talk, and I am supplied with original creative ideas which bless the salesmen, our customers, and everyone concerned. Infinite Intelligence thinks, speaks, and acts through me, and all who are present at my talk are richly blessed with every good and perfect gift coming from the Father of Light."

This sales manager told me that since he began tithing some of his time to God, he has given the best talks of his life, and recently, as a result of his excellent work, he has been made executive vice president of his multi-million dollar corporation.

An Engineer Tithes and Turns the Tide

A chemical engineer, who is vice president of the corporation for which he works, recently told me that one company for whom they supplied certain research products owed his firm $10,000, which no one had been able to collect.

He told me that he had visited his customer and given him a transfusion of faith in himself. The engineer added, "I let him know that we trusted him, believed in him, and knew that he would be able to pay us in full. I invited him out to dinner and told him that we respected his integrity and honesty and that he had been prompt and faithful in all his dealings with us for over twenty years. I also told him that our faith and confidence in him had never diminished and that I personally was praying for his prosperity, growth, and expansion along all lines."

A week passed, and he received a letter from the customer stating that he actually had been contemplating bankruptcy, but that "you have given me back my confidence and faith in myself; I again believe in myself and in my ability to accomplish. The tide has turned, and my customers who previously had been slow to pay, have now paid me. Now I am paying you in full!"

The vice president had praised, blessed, and lifted up this man, whose heart responded to the faith and confidence of the vice president. The financial point was correspondingly harmonious.

How an Artist Tithed for Beauty

A distinguished artist once told me of the marvelous results he got by tithing for beauty. He tithed regularly as follows: "God is indescribable beauty, absolute harmony, and boundless love. The infinite beauty of the Infinite One flows through my mind majestically and gloriously, and my fingers are Divinely guided to portray on the canvas beauty, order, symmetry, and proportion. Everything I paint on my canvas will be a thing of beauty and a joy forever. Every scene and every picture will stir up the gift of God in man."

He gave his tithe (idea of beauty) to his subconscious mind, and the latter thereupon magnified and multiplied whatever was impressed upon it. He impregnated it with beauty, and his subconscious responded, enabling him to bring forth marvelous paintings. Do you think he had any trouble in selling his works at a top price?

How She Tithed for Love

A retired school teacher was living in California, and became acquainted with a great number of other retirees who were constantly declaring how lonesome they were and how frustrated and unhappy they were because, on their low pensions, they could not travel and do the things they wished to do. She decided to avoid falling into that limited state of thought. For several nights in her prayer sessions she tithed as follows:

"God's love fills my soul, and I radiate love and goodwill to all those around me and to all people everywhere. God's love flows through me as harmony, love, companionship, wealth, and true expression. God is my shepherd, and I shall never want for money, love, beauty, or companionship. God answers me now, and I give thanks."

After a few weeks, she was invited to be a companion and interpreter for a wealthy woman who was going to travel extensively and conduct business in France, Germany, and Switzerland. Her knowledge of German and French, previously limited to teaching, proved a great asset, and she was paid handsomely for her services. She wrote me, saying that she was having *the time of her life* and that the assignment was permanent, as her employer considered her to be indispensable. This lady tithed unselfishly, and she was abundantly repaid beyond her expectations. Her secret is now your secret.

The Law of Giving and Receiving

The more love and goodwill you give, the more you will receive. The law of tithing inevitably causes whatever we give out—whether it be goodwill or ill will—to come back to us, often multiplied many times over. It is the immutable law that like attracts like, and that whatsoever you sow in your subconscious that you also shall reap on the screen of space as conditions, experiences, and events.

Give Freely and Joyously

The amount of money donated does not necessarily have to be one-tenth. The one-tenth mentioned in the Bible means a percentage, the idea of the amount you arrive at in your own mind, that which you want to give cheerfully and freely.

For example, suppose that you give five dollars every Sunday to the spiritual activity of your choice; it should be given freely, joyously, lovingly, and with a sense of abandonment, knowing that God is the eternal source of supply and that through Him all your needs are instantaneously met at all times, everywhere. If you should feel a sense of lack or deprivation when you give the five dollars, it would not be a true tithe. To give grudgingly or from a sense of duty or fear is not tithing. On the contrary, such a mental attitude would attract lack to you.

How Your Tithe Multiplies Exceedingly

When you donate regularly, select a sum which you feel in your heart that you want to give, and affirm quietly or audibly: "I release this money freely, and God multiplies it exceedingly."

As you do this, you are depositing the idea of great wealth in your subconscious, which will magnify your wealth in countless ways. This is the meaning of the quotation in the Bible:

Give, and it shall be given unto you; good measure, pressed down, and shaken together, and running over, shall men give into your bosom. For with the same measure that ye mete withal it shall be measured to you again. (Luke 6:38.)

Increase Your Income by Leaps and Bounds

Give to worthy causes regularly, without any strings attached. When contributing the amount you feel you want to give and love to give, then you are really tithing from a sound financial standpoint. As you start off with this correct and dynamic attitude, you will find yourself wanting to give more and more, gladly and happily, because your income goes ahead by leaps and bounds, in even a greater degree, based on the law of giving and receiving.

You blessed your gift and you released it with joy, and your subconscious mind magnified it a thousand-fold. This really is the key to magnifying the wealth of those who regularly tithe.

They are making use of a law of Infinite Mind which works for them—whether or not they know it.

How He Tithed for Supply

A businessman recently said to me, "There's plenty of money in the world—there's plenty of everything; and I know there are endless resources in my subconscious mind that I have never tapped. This is how I personally tithed for supply: I affirmed frequently, 'God is my invariable source of supply, meeting instantly all my needs, and His riches flow to me ceaselessly, tirelessly, and endlessly.' "

As he reiterated these truths, he conveyed to his subconscious mind the idea of riches and wealth flowing to him in avalanches of abundance. This is also your path to financial success.

He Tithed but Did Not Prosper

Some time ago, a man told me that he had tithed regularly to his church, but that he had not prospered. I discovered, however, that he had not completely released his weekly tithe and that in actual fact he felt he was depleting his income by giving to his church. He had mental reservations. After our conference, he reversed his mental attitude and thereafter gave with joy and rich blessings. He soon found that the law of increase works for him also.

I also explained to him that tithing, as understood in the Bible, does not include giving money to various charities and secular organizations, even though such generosity is laudable and praiseworthy. When money is given as a tithe, it must be for the purpose of spreading abroad the truths of God and to the place where you are receiving spiritual help and inspiration.

He replied with gratitude, "This is the explanation I needed. Now I see clearly what tithing really means."

He Was Tithing in Reverse

One man whom I know bitterly complained to me saying, "I tithe large sums of money every Sunday to a religious group in New York, yet I am always trying to make ends meet."

I discovered that his attitude had been: "I don't expect or want anything back." The Bible says that a man shall decree a thing and it shall come to pass. He had given the order to his subconscious mind, and it implicitly obeyed him.

I explained to him that he had been neutralizing his good, somewhat similarly to planting a seed in the ground and digging it up a little later on, thereby preventing its growth. This man began to see that if a farmer planted seeds in the ground, he automatically would reap a harvest—that is, the law of the soil and the law of the mind are the same. He began *to expect* the law of opulence to work for him, and his financial condition improved in a fabulous way.

Practice Wisdom in Tithing

You should be very careful how you give to relatives or to the poor. It is all right to help them to help themselves, but be sure that you do not rob them of their initiative and of their incentive to stand on their own feet and to overcome their problems to the best of their ability. When people receive help too easily and too frequently, they become dependent and, ultimately, leaners and whiners. The finest thing you can give to them is the knowledge of the law of prosperous thinking.

Be sure that you don't hinder or impede others from expressing and developing their own hidden talents and abilities by unwise giving. Often, the recipient of your unwise giving resents you. He feels obligated and he senses your pity or thoughts of lack about him. He knows that he should be as prosperous and as successful as you are, and he feels guilty because he feels he is sponging from you; this results in his deep sense of guilt and resentment toward the giver.

Give him the knowledge of the laws of mind and the way of the Spirit, and he will never want a bowl of soup or an old suit of clothes or a handout of any kind, because you have revealed to him his capacity to go to the treasure house of the Infinite within him and there to take all the riches given to him from the foundation of time.

You Can Tithe All Day Long

Practice tithing all day long. Pour forth and radiate to all people love, kindness, friendship, laughter, confidence, enthusiasm, and goodwill. You can't give one-tenth of these. These qualities can't be divided or multiplied; they are eternal, ageless, and limitless. These qualities and attributes of God within you never grow old. Moreover, there is no shortage of love, gentleness, kindness, goodness, truth, beauty, peace, and joy—all these are of God, and they are timeless, eternal, and infinite. You can't put anything that is *real* on a percentage basis, not even wealth. But wealth can flow to you in the measure you properly tithe for it.

Pour out the riches of Heaven! Give encouragement, faith, hope, appreciation, and gratitude, and as you continue to tithe in this way, God will pour out His blessings on you, pressed down, shaken together, and running over, and in a very tangible financial way.

Bring ye all the tithes into the storehouse, that there may be meat in mine house, and prove me now herewith, saith the Lord of hosts, if I will not open you the windows of heaven, and pour you out a blessing, that there shall not be room enough to receive it. (Malachi 3:10.)

CHAPTER SUMMARY

Special Points to Remember

1. Tithing means that you dedicate a proportion of your income for truly Infinite and sacred purposes. Tithes also mean your beliefs, convictions, and estimates of yourself which you give to the treasure house within you, namely your subconscious mind. This treasure house gives you financial supply.

2. Tithe for harmonious human relationships by assuming that the action of God is taking place in the mind and heart of the other and that there is a harmonious and Divine solution between you.

3. Devote one-tenth of your time in prayer and meditation prior to a lecture or a conference. God will inspire you, and wonders will happen in your life.

4. You tithe by giving a transfusion of faith and confidence to the other person. Let him know that you believe in him and trust him in all ways, and he will respond accordingly.

5. You can tithe for beauty by knowing that the indescribable beauty of God is manifesting itself through you and that others are inspired and lifted up by your works.

6. You can tithe for love by claiming that God's love fills your soul and by radiating love and goodwill to all. Continue to do this, and many miracles will happen in your life.

7. The more love and goodwill you give to others, the more

you will receive back, multiplied and magnified in countless ways. This can also be counted in money.

8. Give freely, joyously, lovingly, and with a sense of abandonment, and as you do, fabulous wealth inevitably will be yours.

9. Donate generously by affirming as follows: "I release this money freely, and God multiplies it exceedingly."

10. Give regularly the amount you feel in your heart you *want* to give, and you will find that your income increases by leaps and bounds.

11. Tithe for financial supply by realizing: "God is my invariable source of supply, instantly meeting all my needs, and His riches flow to me ceaselessly, tirelessly, and endlessly."

12. When you give, there must be no mental reservations or sense of lack. Give with joy and rich blessings to all.

13. In the same way that a farmer expects to reap a harvest, so should you expect the natural law of tithing to work for you.

14. The finest thing you can give others is the knowledge of the law of prosperous thinking, and they will never want for any good thing in life.

chapter 7

The Rich
Get Richer

THE truly rich are those who know the creative power of thought and who continue to impress their thoughts of abundance and prosperity upon their subconscious mind, which in turn causes the things they think about to be objectified in their experience.

Men get rich by thinking in a certain way; they do not think from appearances, because they know that their sustained and creative thoughts tend to manifest in a corresponding form in their world.

To think of riches, when one is in the condition of poverty or lack, requires sustained and concentrated thought; but he who practices this disciplined thinking inevitably becomes rich, and he can have whatever he wants.

The Bible says, . . . *that unto every one that hath shall be given; but from him that hath not, even that which he hath shall be taken away from him.* (*Luke 19:26.*) A popular way of saying it is "the rich get richer while the poor get poorer."

This simply means that the man who gives attention to the limitless riches of his mind, the source of all experience, will possess more of the world's goods. A seed dropped into the ground produces hundreds more seeds; likewise, the seeds (thoughts) of God's riches for you will magnify and multiply in your experience.

Income Follows Changed Attitude

A real estate operator told me recently that he used to think that money or supply was limited, and that the wealth of the country was cornered and controlled by the very rich families of America. He used to get worked up about it.

Suddenly he realized the fallacy of his way of thinking; he realized that he was blocking the creative flow of riches by his disturbed and warped thinking processes.

Here, in part, is his letter: "Dear Dr. Murphy: I followed your instructions. I erased from my mind the idea of competition. I decided I am here to create and that there are countless billions of dollars worth of gold in the soil of the world, not yet discovered. I know that the day will come when scientists will synthetically create gold and any other metal. I ceased driving sharp bargains, cutting corners, and taking advantage of others because of their ignorance or lack of awareness. I stopped coveting the promotions and riches of others. I decided that I could have anything without taking anything away from others. I have become a producer and a cooperator, instead of a competitor.

"My prayer has been as follows for three months: 'The limitless riches of God are flowing to me as fast as I can receive and use them, and every other man gets richer day by day.' This new attitude has worked miracles in my life, and my income has trebled in three months!"

His Multimillion Dollar Formula

A drug magnate who had founded an extensive chain of drug stores was a very spiritual man. He had started an ethical pharmacy in one room in a building and from that humble beginning had founded what eventually became a multimillion dollar business employing thousands. One day during lunch, he took a small card out of his wallet and gave it to me, saying, "This is my Multimillion Dollar Formula. I have been using it night and morning for twenty-five years, and I have given it to many men who also have become actual millionaires as well as to others who have acquired all the money they needed to use freely and joyously."

Here is his formula:

"I recognize the eternal source of all riches which never fails. I am Divinely guided in all my ways, and I adapt myself to all new ideas. Infinite Intelligence is constantly revealing to me better ways to serve my fellow man. I am guided and directed to create products that will bless and help humanity. I attract men and women who are spiritual, loyal, faithful, and talented, and who contribute to the peace, prosperity, and progress of our business. I am an irresistible magnet and attract fabulous wealth by giving the best possible quality of products and services. I am constantly in tune with the Infinite and the substance of wealth. Infinite Intelligence governs all my plans and purposes, and I predicate all my success on the truth that God leads, guides, and governs me in all my undertakings. I am at peace inwardly and outwardly at all times. I am a tremendous success. I am one with God, and God is always successful. I must succeed. I am succeeding now. I grasp the essentials of all details of my business. I radiate love and goodwill to all those around me and to all my employees. I fill my mind and heart with God's love,

power, and energy. All those connected with me are spiritual
links in my growth, welfare, and prosperity. I give all honor and
glory to God."

This business tycoon brought all these things that he affirmed
to pass, and he blessed countless others. . . . *Go, and do thou
likewise (Luke 10:37.)*, and become a multimillionaire blessing
multitudes.

His Block to Riches and the Cure

A real estate salesman said, "I can't figure it out. I work hard
all day long. Clients look at the lots and houses·I have for sale,
but they don't buy. All the other salesmen in the same office are
closing sales every day."

His block was in the inner recesses of his mind. The baneful
emotion he specifically had to overcome was envy. It was the
cause of both his financial lack and his lost sales. He admitted
that he was very envious seeing the other salesmen make large
commissions. He was also deeply resentful.

He was made to understand that his envious thought was the
worst possible attitude to have, for it put him in a very negative
position. As long as he retained this attitude of mind, riches
would flow *from* him instead of *to* him.

His remedy for this state of affairs, he finally discovered, was
to bless all his associates whose more fortunate state had incited
him to envy.

A complete mental cure followed his frequent repetition of
the following prayer, thoughtfully, meaningfully, and knowingly:

"I am aware that there is a perfect law of supply and demand.
I practice the golden rule in all my affairs. I am at peace. Whatever I wish to sell is an idea in the Mind of God. The principle
of all knowledge is within me. I know everything that I need
instantly. I recognize whatever I wish to buy or sell represents
an exchange of ideas in Divine Mind within me. I know that

there are mutual satisfaction, harmony, and peace. The price is right; the people are right; all is in perfect order. I know the Truth; I understand the Truth; and I am the consciousness of God in action. All the ideas I need constantly unfold within me with perfect sequence and perfect combinations. I receive and rejoice in Divine ideas, and I give them to my fellow creatures; I receive ideas in exchange. Peace is mine now. There is no delay in Divine Mind; I accept my good."

I have seldom seen a man so completely transformed spiritually, mentally and financially! He became one of the foremost salesmen in his office. He became kinder, nobler, and more affable and gracious, and his kindness and warmth were genuine. Sales came much faster for him. He discovered that by blessing others, he also blessed himself, and all sense of inferiority and lack were overcome.

How Riches Flow to His Organization

An engineer friend of mine told me that he has a principle of advancement for every employee in his organization. At meetings he tells them constantly that they will share in the growth of the organization and that all who work diligently and harmoniously may advance rapidly. He said that his business is a ladder, which every employee who has the zeal, industry, and willingness may climb to riches, and that if he does not do so it is his own fault.

From time to time, all employees are made aware of the progress of the company, and they share quarterly in the growth on a pro rata basis. He has not had any change in personnel in years and has developed an intensely loyal and a most cooperative industrial family. The spirit of cooperation, rather than competition, prevails among the employees. New accounts and new branches are being opened, and riches flow to this engineering firm from all sides.

Bless and Grow Rich

The cause of your straitened circumstances is your state of mind. Believe and recognize that all the resources and wealth of the Infinite are at your disposal and are seeking to find expression through you.

Many persons have the idea or dominant thought that nothing is really theirs and that they must chase after wealth, else they will lose it.

Bless those whose prosperity, success, and vast riches irritate, annoy, or excite your envy, and pray specifically and definitely that they become far more successful, richer, and blessed in every conceivable manner. By so doing you will heal your own state of mind. When you pray that way and sincerely pour out your benedictions and blessings from your heart upon those who have ascended the ladder of life and who apparently are so much richer than you, you will enter the consciousness of one who, possessing all things, pours out of his inner and outer riches abundant gifts upon others.

In others words, by blessing and prospering others, you will be blessed and prospered. This is why the rich get richer and the poor get poorer. The latter are usually envious and hateful, and these negative emotions bring on greater and greater loss of income. It is your state of mind that robs you, and not a malignant fate.

The Universal Bank

A salesman needed an automobile for his new job, but he had no money with which to purchase one. However, he knew how to draw a check on his mental bank.

He told me that after he got the job, he went back to his room and formed the mental image of the car he wanted, with the positive certainty that it would be given him. He said, "I claimed it as already mine, I could feel the steering wheel, and I rubbed my hand over the upholstery."

He struck up an acquaintance with another man in his apartment house who was going to Europe for six months and who said to him, "Use my car until I return, and by that time you will be able to buy a car of your own."

This man's car was exactly the same make and model as the one he earlier had pictured in his mind! Long before his friend returned from Europe, he had acquired sufficient funds to buy his own car. He had known that there was a bank within him upon which he could draw, and he knew its supply is endless and infinite. . . . *It is your Father's good pleasure to give you the kingdom.* (*Luke 12:32.*)

A Prayer to Overcome Envy and Resentment

"I know that all men are my brothers; all of us have a common Father. I wish for everyone health, happiness, abundance, and all the blessings and riches of life. I mean this; I am sincere. I know that what I wish for the other, I also wish for myself, and as I bless the other I am blessing myself. The love of God flows through me to all mankind. I bless all who are richer than I, and I bless those who criticize and speak ill of me. I rejoice to see all my co-workers succeed and prosper. I open the windows of my mind, and I let in the riches of Heaven. I am loving toward all. I pray that God's riches flood the mind and heart of all. I give thanks for His riches now. It is wonderful!"

CHAPTER SUMMARY

Come Back to Base

1. The rich get richer and attract more and more of the world's goods because they build into their mentality a realization of

God's infinite riches. The steady and joyous expectancy of of riches will draw money from all angles to you.

2. The idea of competition limits your supply. Become a producer and a cooperator, and realize that you can have all the riches you want without taking anything from anyone else. As there is no shortage of air, there is no shortage of the infinite riches of the universe.

3. You go where your vision is. Hold a mental picture of what you want to accomplish and back it up with feeling, and it will come to pass.

4. The block to riches is in the inner recesses of your mind. Envy of others will block your flow of riches and will attract misery and penury.

5. Bless others richly, and you will be blessed. The ship that comes home to your brother comes home to you.

6. Let your business be a ladder which enables every employee to climb to riches. You get rich by making others rich and by paying them their true worth.

7. Your subconscious mind is a bank, and, even though you have no money for something you need, or want, you can make a mental image of that certain something you want and feel its reality; and in ways you know not of, it will become a reality for you.

8. Rejoice to see all your co-workers succeed and prosper. Pray daily that you wish that God's riches may flood the minds and hearts of all men everywhere. *Be not thou afraid when one is made rich, when the glory of his house is increased.* (*Psalm 49:16.*)

chapter 8

How to Produce
Tangible Riches

AS we consider and gaze on the prodigality of Nature, we realize that there is an abundance of all things. Nature is lavish, extravagant, and bountiful. Wherever we go in life, we become aware of how great that fullness is. The laws of life are designed to give us unlimited riches, far beyond our daily needs. The Psalmist says, *The earth is the Lord's, and the fullness thereof* . . . (*Psalm 24:1.*) The only shortage that exists is due to the greed, selfishness, fear, and misappropriation by man, but when wise and just methods are used in the cultivation and distribution of Nature's riches, there is more than enough for all of the tangible riches of life.

Riches Can Be Made Tangible

Many years ago I had a most interesting conversation with a dentist in Sydney, Australia, where I was giving a series of lectures on "The Miracles of Your Subconscious Mind." This dentist told me that when he started practicing dentistry, he had "a penny mind," and he found himself attracting only penny-conscious and very thrifty clients because of his own poverty complex.

This is how be brought tangible riches into his life. Walking home one night after my lecture on the power of mental imagery, he began to imagine that all the air around him was filled with pound notes. He felt the air was simply crammed with them. He said that his mental picture was as real and as vivid as the trees outside his door, and he began to fill his pockets with the imaginary notes of all denominations—he said that they seemed tangible and real to him. Suddenly he realized that there was unlimited wealth which could be attracted and appropriated by anyone who had the faith, receptivity, and initiative to contemplate God's riches.

After this experience he attracted a most influential and prosperous clientele, and he actually acquired more patients than he could take care of. His previous stingy and penny-pinching attitude of ultra-frugality had kept the wealthy people away. He had discovered the power of his thought-image to produce tangible riches of all kinds.

Thinking in a Certain Way

If you want an organ or a piano, for instance, I do not mean that all you have to do is to mentally form the picture of an organ or a piano and that the instrument will take form without hands in your room. If you have the money, you will undoubtedly go out and buy one.

Suppose you need a piano to practice on however, and you don't have the money with which to buy it. Think of a lovely piano, see it in your room, in your imagination, run your hands over the keys, touch them, and feel the solidity, naturalness, and tangibility of it all. Move your hands over the surface, and think with positive certainty that the piano is right there. It *is* there in your mind, because the piano was first a thought in the mind of the maker.

After forming the thought of the piano in your mind, claim it as yours now, and know that your subconscious mind will see to it that you receive it in Divine order. The infinite intelligence within your subconscious mind will act in the minds of others, and it eventually will come to pass in ways you know not of.

Thought has caused the creation of all the machines and instruments in the world and is constantly creating additional millions of improved cars, typewriters, computers, radios, television sets, musical instruments, and countless household appliances of all kinds. All these inventions and discoveries and improvements in our machine and space age are brought about by men thinking in a certain, purposeful way.

The Miracle of Make-Believe

Back in 1944, a little Spanish girl lived a few doors away from me. I knew her family well, and occasionally visited at the home of the little girl's parents. She was about eight years of age, and daily went to the local parochial school.

For months she had been asking her parents for a bicycle to ride in Central Park. Her mother's constant answer was: "Stop bothering me. You know there is a war on, and no bicycles are available." She kept on asking, however, much to the annoyance of her parents. This little girl was a typical tom-boy, who fought with the boys in the neighborhood and occasionally got a black eye.

One night I said to the little girl, "Mary, you can get a bicycle, and I know where." Immediately, her eyes began to shine. She was all ears, and she exclaimed, "Where?" The following colloquy took place between us:

Author: "Go to bed immediately and close your eyes. Then imagine clearly that your boy and girl playmates are riding *your bicycle* in Central Park, and just see their smiles! God wants you to share with your playmates who have no bicycle, so that you can make them happy."

Mary: "Oh, all right, if that's what God wants me to do, I agree. But mother said that Santa Claus could not or would not bring me a bicycle this Christmas, and it's only two weeks away!"

Author: "Do what I told you to do. When you're in bed, close your eyes and imagine and feel yourself riding a bicycle in Central Park. Be sure to 'see' your playmates riding the same bicycle one at a time the way I told you previously. See them smiling and laughing and full of fun. You will get your bicycle! God will tell Santa Claus where to find one. Go off to sleep now, sound asleep, deep, deep, sleep."

The following night Mary was with another girl in a variety store at about six o'clock in the evening, when suddenly Mary began to cry. A lady nearby noticed this and, speaking gently, said to her, "Little girl, what is the matter? Did someone hurt you?"

Mary replied, "No, but there was a man at my house last night and he told me that God would tell Santa Claus where to find a bicycle and that I would get it right away. It's getting dark, and there is still no bicycle."

The lady was moved, and she said, "That man had no right to tell you such a thing!" She took the little girl to her apartment nearby and gave her a bicycle, which her daughter, who had died two years before, had used. The lady stated that she had always wanted to give it to a child who loved God.

This is the power of make-believe. . . . *According to your faith be it unto you.* (*Matthew 9:29.*)

Why He Did Not Get Tangible Results

Recently I talked to a man who had gone into bankruptcy. He had lost his home, and was also suffering from arthritis. The more he struggled to overcome his reverses, the more enmeshed he became. He was in a vicious circle. He said to me, "Why don't I get results? I am a church goer, I pray and read the Psalms, and I have done a lot of good. Why is God punishing me?"

It was true that he prayed and attended his church services regularly; yet I discerned the reason he got no tangible results from his prayer life and efforts was that he had hated a business associate for over ten years. He was warped by a vengeful and malicious emotion and was obdurate in his refusal to forgive; he invoked imprecations and maledictions on this associate. This state of mind was his real block.

I explained to him that his thoughts of his associate, since they were hateful, spiteful, and vengeful, generated destructive emotions in his subconscious mind where they got snarled up, and inasmuch as these emotions of hate, jealousy, and vengeance must have an outlet, they came forth as lack and limitation. All this resulted in bankruptcy and bodily disease.

He found an easy remedy by tuning in on God's inner peace and claiming that the God-wisdom within him would bring about a Divine adjustment in His own way and in His own time. He placed his roots in God, the inexhaustible Source, in which everything has its origin. He began daily to bless the man he hated, claiming that God was flowing through him as harmony, health, peace, and abundance. In a few months, the tide turned in his favor and he was carried along on the crest of the wave to prosperity, success, and achievement.

How a War Refugee Got Marvelous Results

A beautiful, charming, spiritually oriented woman comes to hear my lecture every Sunday morning in Los Angeles. She told me a fascinating story about her early life, which was spent amid the most sordid and squalid conditions. She was brought up in a sort of ghetto in Russia, where systematic pogroms of her race took place. Often hungry and half-clad, she had the indomitable urge to go to America, there to study music, burst the bonds of circumstances, and courageously overcome her thralldom.

At the outbreak of war, she volunteered as a nurse in the Russian army. She subsequently was taken prisoner by the Germans; as a prisoner, she ministered to all those in the prison compound. While there she had a constant mental picture of embracing an uncle who was in Los Angeles. In her mind's eye, she would hear him say over and over again, "Welcome to America!" Every night she would lull herself to sleep, hearing the imaginary voice of her uncle saying, "Welcome to America!"

When the American forces of liberation arrived at her camp, she acted as interpreter. She fell in love with an American infantry officer and eventually found her way to the United States. Today she is a wonderful musician and a splendid teacher, and her students love her. She has a marvelous income, lives in a very fine neighborhood, and has all the money she needs to do everything she wants to do. She travels extensively to many parts of the world.

This woman has demonstrated how you can rise from poverty to riches, and she has really reached the heights in personal attainment. She has never allowed resentment, bitterness, or hatred toward others to sear her soul. She knows that there is a power within her that can overcome and triumph over the stringent pressures of the world and lift her to the heights. Her favorite Biblical quotation is, . . . *I bore you on eagles' wings, and brought you unto myself.* (*Exodus 19:4.*)

Three Words Produced Riches

A motion picture actress told me that she had marvelous results in cleansing her mind of wrong ideas and black moods from which she frequently suffered. She would affirm: "Joy, riches, success." She would chant these three words to herself as she attended to routine chores around the house. After repeating these three words for ten or fifteen minutes, she would become lifted up and exalted in mind, and whenever she slipped into one of her depressive moods about finances and lack of contracts, she would repeat her song of three words.

She found that these words had tremendous power, as they stand for the invisible powers of her subconscious. She anchored her mind on these substantial realities, and results corresponding to their nature eventually manifested in her life.

She has received one contract after another and has not been idle in the past eight years. She is going from glory to glory.

She had discovered a simple truth, and that is that it was her depressing moods and worry which caused the outer conditions and circumstances of her life. When she changed her mental moods of fear, worry, and depression, the outer circumstances righted themselves.

Begin now to sing her silent song of triumph: "Joy. Riches. Success." Wonders will happen in your life!

God Wants You to Be Rich

The law of life is abundance, not poverty. God is infinite, inexhaustible, endless, the eternal source of supply which creates in profusion. You have an invisible means of support. Because God's resources are infinite, your resources are infinite because you and your Father are one.

God gave you hands with which to play the melody of God and to build beautiful structures, edifices, and temples to His glory and honor. God wants you to express your talents in a wonderful way. God gave you a voice that you might sing His song of love to all. God gave you eyes that you might see tongues in trees, sermons in stones, songs in running brooks, and God in everything.

Your desire to dance is God seeking to reveal to you that this is a universe of dancing forces. The whole world is a dance of God.

Your desire to paint a sunset is the indescribable beauty of God seeking expression through you, the artist. God gave you ears to hear the music of the spheres and His still, small voice which says, *"This is the way; walk ye in."*

Your desire to travel and to explore the world is God prompting you and urging you to explore the wonders of the world and to appreciate the beauty, order, symmetry, rhythm, and proportion of all things.

God wants you to be happy, joyous, and free. God wants you to live in a luxurious home and to be clothed beautifully. God wants you to live life gloriously and triumphantly.

. . . *It is God which worketh in you both to will and to do . . .*, said Paul. (*Philippians 2:13.*)

Your desire for riches is the Infinite revealing His riches to you and saying to you, . . . *Son, thou art ever with me, and all that I have is thine.* (*Luke 15:31.*)

CHAPTER SUMMARY

Think on These Things

1. Nature is lavish, extravagant, and bountiful. The laws of life are designed to give you unlimited riches.
2. If you have a "penny-mind" attitude, you will attract people with a poverty complex, and never grow rich.
3. Think clearly of what you want; see it in your room; with

your imaginary hands feel the naturalness, solidity, and tangibility of it, and you will receive it.

4. When you mentally accept something as true, your subconscious mind brings it to pass in ways you know not of, in the same way that a complete stranger gave a bicycle as a present to a little girl who was praying for one.

5. Thoughts of hate, spite, and vengeance will block your prayer for riches and will cause wealth to flow *from* you instead of *to* you. Wish for everyone what you wish for yourself—that is the key to your abundance.

6. There is a multimillion dollar formula. Reiterate these truths feelingly, knowingly, and persistently, and you will have all the riches you need all the days of your life, and you will prosper beyond your fondest dreams.

7. Three words work wonders. Sing them and write them in your heart: "Joy. Riches. Success." These are true of God, and they are also true of you.

8. God wants you to be happy, rich, joyous, and free. God wants you to lead the life more abundant. In Him there is fulness of joy. In Him there is no darkness at all.

chapter 9

All Business
Is God's Business

ALL forms of activity in this world are a part of the omni-action of God. There is only one Supreme Power activating and animating all things and all people. You may speak of spiritual and secular activities, but all work really is spiritual when you love what you are doing, and when you are doing it for the glory and honor of God.

A carpenter who builds a house according to universal principles and who loves what he is doing and rejoices in giving good service is doing spiritual work, just as much as a minister is when expounding on the meaning of the Ten Commandments.

If you make a better razor blade, shaving cream, automobile, or what not, your desire is to serve others joyously and to contribute to humanity in some useful and constructive way, and to practice the golden rule in all transactions. You are about God's business, and God, by His very nature, is for you; who then can be against you? Then there is no power in heaven or on earth that can withhold from you success and prosperity in business.

Prosperity Prayer for Business

"I know and believe that my business is God's business. God is my partner in all my affairs; to me this means that His light, love, truth, and inspiration fill my mind and heart in all ways. I solve all of my problems by placing my complete trust in the Divine power within me. I know that this Presence sustains everything. I now rest in security and in peace. This day I am surrounded by perfect understanding; there is a Divine solution to all my problems. I definitely understand everyone; I am understood. I know that all my business relationships are in accord with the Divine law of harmony. I know that God indwells all of my customers and clients. I work harmoniously with others to the end that happiness, prosperity, and peace will reign supreme."

God Is the True Employer

A young lady working for a large continental organization said, "I used to wander from job to job and from one employer to another, trying to make more money and to improve myself. Since I started affirming and realizing that God is my true employer and that I am working for Him, and that God gave me all riches to enjoy, I got a wonderful position with a wonderful income, and I have been there for six years. I am now engaged to the executive vice president. It is the most wonderful thing in all the world to realize that God is the only employer and that you are not working for man but for God. I now laugh, sing, and rejoice in my work, and I feel secure and at peace. It is wonderful!"

How to Find the Real Boss

Some years ago, a pharmacist visited me in Dallas, Texas. His complaint was that his boss was crotchety, petulant, cantankerous, and generally impossible to get along with. He said, "The only reason I stay there is because the pay is good; but I resent and hate him him so much that I am burning up inside! Moreover, all the other assistants have been promoted in the organization but me."

This young man had installed dictators, despots, and gangsters in his own mind in the form of smoldering anger, resentment, and hate. This destructive attitude of mind governed and controlled him and was boss over his thoughts, feelings, and reactions.

I explained to him that the outside always mirrors the inside, that he was hurting himself and impeding his financial and professional advancement, and that his resentment and hostility paid no dividends. He quickly perceived that the way he felt inside was determined by the way he was thinking. He therefore reversed his mental attitude and established the ideas of success, harmony, and prosperity in his mind. He began to live with these ideas and he nourished them regularly and systematically in his mind; he also purposefully and sincerely wished harmony, peace, and happiness to his employer.

After a few weeks he found that his new attitude was his real boss and that the control of his life definitely was based on the ideas enthroned in his mind. He shortly discovered that his employer's attitude toward him had changed. His employer promoted him and made him manager of one of the branch stores with a big increase in salary. His changed attitude had obviously changed everything!

A Secret of Success in Salesmanship

I have just finished talking with a young salesman whose income averages over $25,000 yearly. He pointed out that his primary thought in selling is *service,* and that he always tries to make money for his customer—or to save him money—and that he never takes advantage of a customer in any way whatsoever. He further declared that he never tries to "load" his customers with merchandise which he feels the buyer cannot really use or sell.

When he cannot furnish or supply the needs of a customer, he said that he always refers him to another manufacturer who has what the customer wants. "This," he said, "is simply the golden rule in action." All his customers appreciate it beyond words! He has lost many orders by this attitude, but he has gained hundreds in their place, and his annual sales figure exceeds any other salesman in the company.

This young man's sincerity, honesty, and goodwill are communicated to the subconscious of his clients, begetting confidence and trust in return. His practice of the golden rule is the secret of his success in salesmanship, as well as of his subsequent promotion to an executive level.

The real secret is to treat your customer exactly as you would like him to treat you, if the tables were reversed. Tell your client, customer, or the purchaser of your home or land, what you yourself would like to be told if you were buying the merchandise or the land; if you do this, the whole world and all the people therein contained will be constrained to do you good, and you will be a fabulous success as a salesman.

Your Voice Can Be God's Voice

I knew a young boy, aged seventeen, who was born in a place in New York called "Hell's Kitchen." He listened to some lectures I gave many years ago in New York. He had a wonderful voice, but it was not cultivated or professionally trained. I told him that the image to which he gave attention in his mind would be developed in his deeper mind and would come to pass, and that there was always a response by this deeper mind to the mental picture held in his conscious mind.

This young man would sit down quietly in his room at home, relax his whole body, and vividly imagine himself singing before a microphone. He would actually reach out for the "feel" of the instrument. He would affirm boldly, "My voice is God's voice, and I sing majestically and gloriously." He would hear me congratulate him on his wonderful contracts and tell him how magnificent his voice was. By giving his attention and devotion to the mental image regularly and systematically, a deep impression was made on his subconscious mind.

A short time elapsed, and a prominent voice instructor in New York offered to give him free lessons several times a week, because he said that the boy's possibilities were great. Eventually, the young man signed a contract whereby he was provided the opportunity to go abroad to sing in the salons of Europe, Asia, South Africa, and elsewhere. His financial worries were over, for he also received a wonderful income.

His hidden talents and ability to release them however, were his *real* riches. His business was God's business, inasmuch as his natural endowment to sing was God-given. Your voice can be God's voice in your daily routines if you will but release its Infinite power.

A Sure Way to Expand Your Prosperity

A minister friend of mine once told me that in his early days he and his church suffered financially. He eventually discovered a sure way to expand and to prosper. He asked himself these two questions: "How can I be more useful to my fellow man?" and, "How can I contribute more to humanity?"

This is the technique or process he used, which worked wonders for him: He affirmed prayerfully and lovingly, "God reveals to me better ways to present the truths of God to my fellow man." Money began to pour in, the mortgage on his church was paid off in a few months, and he has never worried since about money.

Likewise, you will never have to worry about money for your business expansion if you will enthrone in your mind: "God reveals to me better ways in which I can serve my fellow man." New and creative ideas will come to you, and your business will prosper along all lines.

How One Person Got to Head a $200 Million Corporation

Following a lecture in Phoenix, Arizona, a man chatted with me and said that when he had been sales manager of a certain organization, he suffered a nervous breakdown, plus a cardiac attack due to pressure, strain, tension, and "political" strife within the organization.

When he had fully recuperated, however, and had returned to his office, he adopted the following procedure: Every morning he would close his office door and spend ten or fifteen minutes communing and conversing with God. He claimed that infinite intelligence was directing all his activities for the day, that Divine love and harmony prevailed where discord was, and that his judgment, decisions, and purchases would be governed by the wisdom of God anointing his intellect, which would reveal the perfect plan and show him the way he should go. He would boldly claim that God knew all the answers to all his problems and that he was one with God. When he called upon this Supreme Wisdom, it always answered him. He claimed boldly: "Divine law and order govern me, the board of directors, and the entire organization. I radiate love, peace, prosperity, and goodwill to all."

Following this procedure, he never missed a day at work and was healthier and happier in every way. New creative ideas for expansion and promotion of the company's products continuously came to him. As a consequence the business prospered beyond his fondest dreams. He moved up the executive ladder, and within two years he was elected president of an enormous corporation at a fabulous salary.

He had proved to himself that God's business always prospers. You can do the same for yourself.

Today Is Not Mortgaged

If you can't meet the mortgage today, if you find yourself unable to pay certain bills, or if you anticipate failure today, remember that all you have to do is to change your present thought, and you will change conditions. You always are experiencing the outward picturing of your mind's activity at every moment. What is happening to you today is the result of today's thinking and feeling.

Think rightly today—the future is always the present thought made manifest. Change your thinking today, and you can make it harmonious, peaceful, and successful.

Your trouble today is the result of today's thinking. In Divine Mind, there is no time or space. Your good is literally this present moment. The past is a present thought; the future also is a present thought, because you can think only in the NOW. You live this moment. Change this moment, and you change your destiny! The only moment you have control of is this present moment. This is why the ancient Hindu mystics said, "God (your good) is the Eternal Now."

Three Steps to Business Success

A young lady operated a very beautiful hair salon. Her mother became ill, however, and she had to devote considerable time at home, necessarily neglecting her business. During her absence, two of her assistants embezzled funds, and she found herself deeply in debt.

She decided to use the following three steps to recoup her business losses:

First step: She began to imagine that the local bank manager was congratulating her on her wonderful deposits in the bank. She kept imagining in this manner for about five minutes at a time.

Second step: In her imagination, she heard her mother saying to her, "I am so happy that you are doing so well and that you have such wonderful customers!" She continued to hear her mother say this in a happy, joyous way for about three to five minutes.

Third step: Just before going to sleep, she affirmed: "I am giving loving service to everyone, and God is blessing everyone in my salon through me."

In less than three weeks, her business began to boom, and she had to hire additional operators. In the meantime, she got married, and her husband gave her $20,000 as a wedding gift with which she enlarged her business and opened new facilities.

The Truth About Buying and Selling

I am frequently consulted about buying and selling in connection with real estate, buildings, and stores; actually, it applies to any commodity which you might wish to buy or to sell. When you wish to sell, it means that you are ready to pass on your property or home because you wish to change; it also means that someone else is ready to receive.

In buying or selling, realize that you are instantly in touch with the right buyer or seller at the right time, and your subconscious mind will bring both of you together. You are operating a law of attraction, and you will find yourself doing business with a person who is perfectly satisfied with the transaction; everything will be in Divine order.

The price you are asking is always right and just, when, if the situation were reversed, you would be willing to pay the same price yourself.

Daily Affirmations for Financial Success

... *Wist ye not that I must be about my Father's business?* (*Luke 2:49*) "I know that my business, profession, or activity is God's business. God's business is always basically successful. I am growing in wisdom and understanding every day. I know, believe, and accept the fact that God's law of abundance is always working for me, through me, and all around me.

"My business or profession is full of right action and right expression. The ideas, money, merchandise, and contacts that I need are mine now and at all times. All these things are irresistibly attracted to me by the law of universal attraction. God is the life of my business; I am Divinely guided and inspired in all ways. Every day I am presented with wonderful opportunities to grow, expand, and progress. I am building up goodwill. I am a great success, because I do business with others as I would have them do it with me."

CHAPTER SUMMARY

Serve Yourself with Good Business Thoughts

1. All business is God's business, and God's business always prospers. Do all things gladly and joyously for the glory of God.

2. Realize that God is your partner in all your business transactions and that He indwells all your customers and clients,
   and you will be guided and directed in all your ways.

3. Realize that God is your only Employer. As you do this,
   you will always be gainfully employed and have a deep,
   abiding sense of security.

4. Your dominant mental attitude is your real boss. Ideas are
   our masters and determine our attitudes. Enthrone in your
   mind the ideas of harmony, success, and prosperity, and
   nourish them emotionally; you will find that, having a good
   boss inside, the same will appear on the outside.

5. To succeed in salesmanship, you must have service to the
   customer as your primary goal; then success is assured.

6. If you are endowed with the gift of song in your heart,
   realize your voice is God's voice and that your singing
   thrills and blesses the audience. This is the sure way to
   fame and glory.

7. If business is slow, pray as follows: "Infinite Intelligence
   reveals to me better ways in which I can serve." Your business will go ahead by leaps and bounds!

8. Your experiences today are not caused by yesterday, but
   are an out-picturing of your present thought. Change your
   thought now, and you change everything. The only moment
   is *now*. The future is determined by your *present* thought.

9. In buying and selling, realize that you are instantly in touch
   with the right buyer or seller at the right time. The law of
   attraction will bring both of you together, and there will be
   mutual satisfaction, harmony, and peace in your transaction.

chapter 10

The Law
of Increase

IN *I Corinthians 3:6* we read: *I have planted, Apollos watered; but God gave the increase.* Increase is what all men and women throughout the world are seeking; it is the urge of God within them, seeking fuller expression in all phases of their lives.

Your desire to grow wealthy, to expand, and to unfold is a fundamental impulse of your being. You wish to increase your circle of wonderful friends, you wish more and better food, clothing, automobiles, and homes, and more of the luxuries of life. Moreover, you desire to travel more, to learn more of the inner powers, and to experience a greater measure of beauty. In short, you want to live the life more abundant.

You plant wheat in the soil and water the ground, but God gives the increase in the form of multiplying the wheat grains a hundred-fold or a thousand-fold. Likewise, whatever you plant in your mind in the way of thought, feeling, and imagination is increased in manifestation.

Increase means the multiplication of your good, the unfolding of your incipient thought or plan. If no action is initiated, obviously there can be no increase. Begin now to impress your mind with the idea of increase. You can't do it alone, however; it is God that giveth the increase.

How One Idea Attracted Thousands of Dollars

Dr. Olive Gaze, wife of the late Dr. Harry Gaze, famous international lecturer on The Psychology of Daily Living, has given me this interesting anecdote regarding her late husband.

Dr. Gaze was a very young man when he arrived from England in order to lecture in the United States. He had decided to lecture in Chicago on the laws of mind. His hotel was near the Chicago Opera House, and as he looked out the window, he saw a large crowd pouring out of the building after a matinee performance. He said to himself, "I am going to speak on the laws of mind to a capacity audience in that Opera House. God will bless me and all those who listen to me with the blessed increase, 'pressed down, and shaken together and running over.' "

Dr. Gaze had only a hundred dollars when he went to see the manager of the Opera House in order to rent it for lectures on The Psychology of Daily Living. The manager laughed, but as Dr. Gaze talked about the powers of the mind, the manager became intensely interested and told him he would give him a week to collect the several thousand dollars necessary for rental of the Opera House for his series of lectures.

During the course of the week, Dr. Gaze kept on affirming, "God giveth the increase. This idea of mine is good; it blesses all. God magnifies it and multiplies it."

Dr. Gaze then met Mr. McCormick of Chicago, a multimillionaire who became intensely interested in Dr. Gaze's mental therapeutics, and he gave a luncheon for him, inviting eleven guests, all also millionaires. Dr. Gaze addressed them on the powers of the mind. The result was that each one contributed a large amount of money and thereby paid for all the necessary advertising, as well as the large sum necessary for the rental.

Dr. Gaze's dream had come true. Crowds could be seen leaving the Opera House after each of his lectures, just as he had imagined from his hotel window a few weeks previously. Dr. Gaze had planted the mental picture in his mind, accompanied by a feeling of joy and restfulness in foreseeing the accomplishment of his idea, while knowing in his heart that God giveth the increase.

How a School Teacher Gives Increase to all Students

A school teacher who regularly comes to my lectures told me that she used to have great trouble with unruly children in school. However, she adopted the following procedure with remarkable and amazing results.

For fifteen minutes every morning before she started class, she isolated herself, became quiet in her mind, and silently affirmed as follows: "I am a creative center of God, and I give increase of love, wisdom, and understanding to all the boys and girls in my class. I am now conveying the idea of advancement and growth to each pupil. I have the unshakeable faith that each pupil learns quickly and is inspired, harmonious, loving, and most cooperative. I have the firm conviction that each child in my class is an advancing student, and my conviction is conveyed to his subconscious mind. It is so."

In the years that followed, this teacher has been complimented time and time again on the order and discipline in her classes, and the grades of her pupils are exceptionally good. Recently she has been promoted and transferred to another school with a big increase in salary. She claimed continuous increase for herself and for her pupils, and she has found that in giving increase to all her pupils God has blessed them as well as herself.

She has a motto on her desk which reads: "What I want for myself, I want for everybody." It really paid off for her.

From Cabin Carpenter to Skyscraper Builder

Recently, I returned from lecturing in Phoenix, Arizona, where I spoke in the Church of Divine Science conducted by Dr. Jacob Sober, formerly a distinguished Rabbi who is now conducting non-denominational services on mental and spiritual laws.

While lecturing there, I chatted with a man who told me that twenty years ago, he had been a carpenter doing odd jobs in that desert town. He had lived in an old, dilapidated cabin on the nearby mountain. However, he had felt an unquenchable desire to build skyscrapers comparable to those in New York City. He began to say to himself, "I am getting rich, I am making others very rich, and I am conferring blessings on all."

Following this changed attitude of mind, he began to attract men and women who wanted his services. His carpentry business increased so rapidly that he couldn't handle it and he had to hire additional men.

He built a house for a very rich man who came from the East for the benefit of his health. As a result of his excellent work, this man set him up in business as a contractor, retaining a small interest in the business. When the wealthy man eventually passed on, he left sole ownership to the carpenter. Today, this former carpenter is worth many millions of dollars and already has built several skyscrapers.

Begin now to feel rich like this carpenter, and you will be amazed at the unexpected blessings which will come to you from all sides. You will be able to expand into larger business combinations, and inevitably with God's help you will receive all the wealth you need for your plans to move onward and upward.

No matter who you are or what you are doing—whether you are a stenographer, secretary, lawyer, chemist, taxi driver, or clergyman—if you begin now to focus your mind on the thought of wealth, health, and happiness for others, they will sense it subconsciously and will be attracted to you by the universal law of attraction. You will become fabulously rich and will prosper spiritually, mentally, and materially.

Why People Beat a Path to His Door

A young physician whom I know astonished his confreres by his phenomenal success. Patients come to him in throngs! He told me that the first day he opened his office, he meditated as follows: "I give increase of life to others. God is the Great Physician and I am His instrument; He heals through me. Everyone I touch is miraculously healed, and I am constantly in tune with the Infinite Healing Presence. I give thanks for my success, achievement, and for the riches of life."

Every day he prays in the above manner. He cannot handle the number of patients who come to him and he has to refer many of them to other doctors.

How Renewal of Mind Benefited a Minister

Recently I talked with a minister whose congregation had fallen down to about fifty or sixty people. During the conference we determined that the reason for the deterioration was that he was not giving them what they wanted or needed.

He forthwith reversed his attitude of mind and began to teach people how to lead a full and happy life, how to prosper, how to establish harmonious human relationships, how to love and be loved, how to prosper in business or a profession, and how to be healthy, vital, and inspired. He had realized that he could not have given these qualities to others except they were a part of his own life.

He began to practice what he preached, and he demonstrated the laws of life from his pulpit. In three months' time he has built up his church to over 500. His people tell him, "These are the things we want to hear. We have a new man in the pulpit!"

He has been transformed by the renewal of his mind. This minister has proved that the law of increase is as mathematically certain as are the laws of chemistry, physics, or gravitation.

Perpetual Opportunity for Advancement Exists for You

Some people say that they can't get ahead or be promoted because they are working in a place where there is no opportunity for advancement or where wages are set by certain standards. All this is not necessarily true. You can use the laws of mind to advance and to move forward in life in any circumstances.

The secret is to form a clear mental picture of what you want to be, know that the power and wisdom of your subconscious will back you up, and persevere and be determined to be what you want to be. Have faith that your mental picture will be developed in your subconscious mind and become objectified in your experience.

Love what you are doing now, i.e., do the best you can where you are. Be cordial, kind, affable, and full of goodwill. Think big and think of riches, and your present work will simply be a stepping stone to your triumph. Be conscious of your true worth, and claim riches in your mind and claim riches for every single person you meet during the day, whether it be your boss, an associate, the foreman, a customer, or a friend—all those around you. You will feel your radiation of riches and advancement, and

Infinite Intelligence will very soon open up a new door of opportunity for you.

There is nothing in all the world to hold you back but yourself, i.e., your own thought and concept of yourself.

When you are seeking and picturing advancement, and when the opportunity for more money and increased status and prestige is presented to you, if you feel receptive to the idea, take it, and it will prove to be a step toward greater and grander opportunities. Enter now into the advancing life and experience the riches of God here and now.

How a Businessman Overcame His Negative Thinking

A woman once complained to me that her husband was constantly blaming the government, the taxes, and the competitive system for his lack of sufficient money.

In talking to him, I discovered that he thought he was a victim of conditions, instead of master of his situation. He began to realize, however, that he could enter upon a creative plan of thinking which would transcend his environment and condition and that he was a citizen of the Kingdom of God. His daily prayer was as follows:

"The law of increase is inevitable, and my mind is constantly open to a bountiful increase. My business grows, expands, and unfolds in a wonderful way, and my finances are always multiplied exceedingly. I am richly and abundantly supplied within and without from the infinite storehouse within me. I open my mind and my heart to the abundance and riches of God, and I am increasingly rich within and without."

As he fed his mind with these inner truths, his outer supply became more abundant. He is now in business for himself and is exceedingly prosperous.

CHAPTER SUMMARY

Think on These Things

1. Increase is what all men are seeking. It is the urge of God seeking expression through you, telling you to come on up and to rise to a higher level.

2. Plant a mental picture in your mind, accompanied by a feeling of joy and restfulness, and contemplate the happy ending, and you will experience the joy of the answered prayer.

3. You are a creative center, and you can give an increase of love, wisdom, and understanding to all. As you give, you receive, and wonders will happen in your life.

4. Let these truths sink into your mind; imbibe them with faith and expectancy: "I am getting rich, I am making others rich, and I am conferring blessings on all." This is the royal road to riches.

5. Give increase to others in your thought life and realize that you are an instrument through which God's love, truth, beauty, and riches flow. Claim that these qualities are constantly flowing through others, also, and you will attract riches, friends, customers, clients, and marvelous experiences.

6. If you are a minister, teach people the abundant life and how to realize it, teach them the laws of prosperity and the science of happy, joyous, and successful living, and there will not be an empty seat in your church.

7. Opportunities are always knocking at your door. Form a clear mental picture of what you want to be and feel and know that the power of your subconscious will bring it to pass. This is your opportunity now!

8. There is no one to blame but yourself. Cease blaming the government, taxes, competition, and world conditions. You are a citizen of infinite mind and infinite riches! Think big, picture riches, and feel that you are rich—and the law of attraction will do the rest.

chapter II

Mental Imagery
and Riches

NAPOLEON once said, "Imagination rules the world"; and Henry Ward Beecher in a similar vein said, "The soul without imagination is what an observatory would be without a telescope."

Imagination is one of the primal faculties of your mind. It has the power to project and to clothe your ideas, giving them visibility on the screen of space. Imagination is the mighty instrument used by great scientists, artists, physicists, inventors, business tycoons, and writers. Scientists, through their imagination, penetrate the depths of reality and are enabled to reveal the secrets of nature.

When the world says, "It is impossible; it can't be done," the man with disciplined, controlled, and directed imagination says, "It *is* done!"

It is just as easy—and far more interesting, captivating, and alluring—for you to imagine yourself to be rich and successful as it is to dwell on poverty, penury, and failure. If you wish to bring about the realization of your desires or ideals, form a mental picture of fulfillment in your mind; constantly imagine the reality of your desire. In this way, you will actually force it into being.

What you imagine as true already exists in your mind, and if you remain faithful to your ideal it will one day objectify itself. The Master Architect within you will project on the screen of visibility that which you impress on your mind.

He Imagined a Million-Dollar Business

An outstanding businessman during a casual conversation told me how he had started in a small store, but that regularly and systematically over the years he used to picture himself as head of a large corporation with branches all over the country. For ten or fifteen minutes in the morning, the afternoon, and at night, he would picture in his mind's eye the giant buildings, factories, and stores, while knowing that through the alchemy of the mind, he would weave the fabric out of which his dream would be clothed.

Gradually, his business began to boom, and he had to enlarge his store and to open other branches. He began to attract to himself by a universal law of attraction the ideas, personnel, friends, money, and everything else he needed for the complete unfoldment of his ideal.

He truly and sincerely exercised and cultivated his imagination and he lived with his mental patterns until his imaginative faculties clothed them in form. Today he is fabulously wealthy and is president of a corporation which employs thousands of people.

She Created Riches for Her Brother

A student at the University of Southern California heard me explain that one of the meanings of *Joseph* in the Bible is *imagination* and that the Bible says *he wears a coat of many colors*. Biblically speaking, a *coat* is a psychological covering. Your psychological "garments" are the mental attitudes, moods, and feelings that you entertain. Joseph's *coat of many colors* represents the many facets of the diamond, or your capacity to clothe any idea in form.

The student began to imagine her brother, who was very poor, as living in the lap of luxury. She pictured his face lighting up with joy, his expression changing, and a broad smile crossing his lips. She imagined that he was telling her what she wanted to hear, such as "Sis, I'm wealthy, successful, and happy. I feel wonderful! I have a new car and a lovely apartment, and I am rolling in riches!"

She was faithful to her mental picture night and morning, and she made it vivid and real until she succeeded in impregnating her subconscious with her mental movie. By the end of two months, her brother had been offered a wonderful position; the company for which he worked had given him a car for business purposes, and he had won a large sum of money in a lottery! This girl had the joy, the thrill and the satisfaction of hearing her brother telling her objectively what she had felt to be true subjectively.

You can imagine abundance and riches where there is lack; peace where there is discord; and health where there is sickness. Imagination disposes of everything; it creates riches, beauty, justice, and happiness, which are everything in this world.

Imagining Success in Financial Matters

A business friend of mine once had difficulty in collecting $10,000 owed him for merchandise by one of his old customers. My friend had pleaded with the man for over two years, but he had received nothing but unfulfilled promises to pay. He hesitated to sue this old customer because of their long business association; but he was deeply resentful and angry toward him.

At my suggestion, my friend reversed his attitude toward his customer. He began to imagine and affirm that his customer was honest, sincere, loving, and kind; after a while my friend's reaction changed. He would sit quietly several times daily and imagine a check for $10,000 to be in his hand, and he would picture himself in a very vivid form depositing the check in his local bank. He also sat down and wrote his customer an imaginary letter of thanks for having paid his debt; he sealed the letter and placed it in a drawer in his desk.

He knew that he was giving a definite picture to his subconscious mind, and he also was aware that the subconscious would bring it to pass. In ten days, he received an envelope from his customer, enclosing the $10,000 check, to which was appended this note: "You have been in my mind the last few days. I felt I must pay you in full. I regret the delay; some day I'll explain." This proves that a changed mental picture changes everything.

Imagination Pours Forth Riches

It is really out of the imaginative mind of man that television, radio, radar, superjets, and all modern inventions come. Your imagination is the treasure house of Infinity, which releases to you all the precious jewels of music, art, poetry, and discoveries.

Consider for a moment a distinguished, talented architect. He builds in his mind a beautiful, modern, twentieth century city for senior citizens, complete with swimming pools, aquarium, recreation centers, parks, etc. He can construct in his mind the most beautiful palace the human eye has ever seen. He can visualize the buildings in their entirety, completely erected before he ever gives his plans to the builders. His inner riches create outer riches for himself and for countless others.

You are the architect of your future. You could now look at an acorn and, with your imaginative eye, construct a magnificent forest full of rivers, streams and rivulets. You could people the forest with all kinds of life; furthermore, you could hang a bow on every cloud. You could look at a desert and cause it to rejoice and blossom as a rose. Men who are gifted with intuition and imagination find water in the desert, and they create cities where formerly other men saw only a desert and a wilderness.

A Fortune in the Desert

About ten years ago, I purchased some land in Apple Valley from a man who told me that in the height of the depression in the early 1930's he and his wife were motoring to Nevada and, in passing through Apple Valley, a vast desert, he said to his wife, "There will be a town here in the near future. Many people will move out here to this desert and build schools, hospitals, homes, and industries. It's Government land; I am going to buy 600 acres."

The price at that time was $2.00 an acre. From an investment of $2.00 an acre, he has made a small fortune. This land is now selling at $400.00 an acre, and possibly more. Countless thousands of men and women had passed through that same area on their way to Nevada. They saw only a desert—he saw a fortune.

The Bible says, ... *I will make the wilderness a pool of water, and the dry land springs of water.* (*Isaiah 41:18.*)

How One Person Successfully Imaged Her Desires

A school teacher who listens to my daily radio program wrote to me, saying that she had written in a notebook the words *Health, Wealth, Love,* and *Expression.* She said that she lacked health and sufficient money, was unmarried, and was seeking opportunity to teach in a college. Under *Health,* she wrote in her notebook: "I am all health; God is my health. Under *Wealth* she wrote: "God's riches are mine now, and I am wealthy." Under *Love* she wrote: "I am happily married and Divinely happy."

Under *Expression* she wrote: "Divine intelligence leads and guides me to my right work, which I perform in a perfect way for a wonderful income."

Every morning and evening, she would look at what she had written in her book, and she claimed: "All these desires are now being fulfilled by my subconscious mind." She would then take some time to picture the complete result under each category. She would imagine her physician as saying to her, "You are completely healed. You are all right now." She would imagine her mother, with whom she lived, saying to her, "You are rich now. We can move and travel. I'm so happy." She would then imagine a minister saying, "I now pronounce you man and wife," and she would "feel" the naturalness, solidity, and tangibility of an imaginary ring being placed on her finger. Prior to sleep, her last mental picture was of her principal saying to her, "Sorry you are leaving, but I am glad to hear of your college assignment. Congratulations!"

She would run each mental movie separately for about five minutes in a completely relaxed and joyous manner, knowing that these pictures would sink down by osmosis into her deeper mind, where they would gestate in the darkness and be made manifest at the right time in the right way. She found all this a most fascinating mental exercise, and her world apparently magically melted into the image and likeness of her disciplined, controlled, and directed daily imagination. Within three months' time, all her desires were fulfilled.

She discovered that there is a designer, an architect, and a weaver within, that takes the fabric of your mind, thoughts, images, feelings, and beliefs, and molds them into a pattern of life which brings you the riches of health, wealth, love, and expression. Her favorite Bible verse is *Psalm 121:1: I will lift up mine eyes* (imagination) *unto the hills, from whence cometh my help.*

You Are Always Imaging

You are constantly using your imagination—either constructively or destructively. You think in mental pictures. Think of your mother and you picture her; think of a home, and you see one in your mind's eye. A poverty stricken person is always imaging lack and limitation of all kinds, and the mind produces according to the mental image held in the mind.

When you were going to get married, you had vivid, realistic pictures in your mind. With your power of imagination, you saw the minister or the priest. You heard him pronounce the words; you saw the flowers and the church, and you heard the music. You imagined the ring to be on your finger, and you travelled in your imagination on your honeymoon to Niagara Falls or to Europe. All this was performed by your imagination.

Likewise, before you graduated, you had a beautiful, scenic drama taking place in your mind; you had clothed in material form all your ideas about graduation. You had imagined a professor or the president of the college giving you your diploma. You saw all the students dressed in gowns. You heard your mother or father or your girl friend congratulate you; you felt their embrace and their kiss. It was all real, dramatic, exciting, and wonderful.

Images appeared freely in your mind as if from nowhere, but you know and must admit there was and is an Internal Creator with power to mold all these forms which you envisioned in your mind, to endow them with life and motion, and to give them voice. These images said to you, "For you only, we live!"

How a Broker Images Riches for Others

A broker friend of mine is intensely interested in making money for his clients. Consequently, he has become very successful and recently has been promoted to the position of executive vice-president of his company. His method is very simple. Prior to coming to his office, he sits still, quiets his mind, relaxes his body, and mentally conducts imaginary conversations with a number of his clients who, one after the other, congratulate him on his wise and sound judgment and also compliment him on his purchases of the right stocks. He dramatizes this imaginary conversation regularly, and he psychologically implants it in his subconscious as a form of belief in his mind.

At intervals during the day, this broker returns to the mental pictures in his mind, thereby making a deep impression on his subconscious mind. He told me that he has made small fortunes for many of his clients and that he has yet to see one lose money due to his advice.

This broker realizes that that which is subjectively embodied is in the natural order of things objectively expressed. It is the *sustained* mental picture which is developed in the depth of the mind. Run your mental movie often. Get into the habit of frequently flashing it on the screen of your mind. After a while, it will become a definite, habitual pattern. The inner movie which you have seen with your mind's eye shall be made manifest openly. In *Romans 4:17* we read, . . . *He calleth the things that are not, as though they were . . .*, and the unseen becomes seen.

The Science of Riches

In the science of imagination, you must first of all begin to discipline your imagination and not let it run riot. *Science insists upon purity*. If you wish a chemically pure product, you must remove all traces of other substances as well as extraneous material; you must cast away all the dross.

In the science of imagination, you eliminate all the mental

impurities, such as envy, covetousness, fear, worry, and jealousy. You must focus all your attention on your goals and objectives in life and refuse to be swerved from your purpose or aim, which is to lead a rich and happy life. Become mentally absorbed in the reality of your desires, and you will see them take material form in your world.

A business man whose affairs are prospering comes home from the office and runs a motion picture in his mind of failure, sees the shelves empty, imagines himself going into bankruptcy and having an empty bank balance. He even imagines the business as closing down, yet all the time he is actually prospering. There is no truth whatever in that negative mental picture of his; it is a lie made out of whole cloth.

In other words, the thing he fears does not exist save in his morbid imagination. The failure will never come to pass—unless he keeps up that morbid picture charged with the emotion of fear. If he constantly indulges in this mental picture, of course, he will bring failure to pass. He has the choice of failure or success, but he is choosing failure.

Enthrone now in your mind the mental images, ideas, and thoughts which heal, bless, prosper, inspire, and strengthen you. It is true that you become what you imagine yourself to be. Your sustained imagination is sufficient to remake your world. Trust the laws of your mind to bring your good to pass, and you will experience all the blessings and riches of life.

CHAPTER SUMMARY

Summary of Your Aids to the Wonders of Imagination

1. "Imagination rules the world." Napoleon.
2. Imagination is one of the primal faculties of your mind,

and has the power to project and to clothe all your ideas into form on the screen of space.

3. If you are in business, you can picture a larger business, new offices, new buildings, and additional stores, and through the alchemy of the mind you can bring these pictures to pass.

4. You can make others rich by seeing them as they ought to be: radiant, happy, joyous, wealthy, and successful. Remain faithful to your mental picture, and it will come to pass. This is blessing the other.

5. If you have difficulty in collecting a debt, picture the check in your hand, feel its reality, and give thanks for the prosperity and success of the person who owes you the money, and miraculously he will pay you.

6. It is out of the imaginative powers of man that come all our new discoveries, such as radio, television, radar, and superjet airplanes. Imagination plumbs the depths of mind, and that which exists in latency is brought forth and projected on the screen of space.

7 When you look at the desert, what do you see? Some people see fabulous riches and they make the desert rejoice and blossom as the rose. Imagination is called the "workshop of God."

8 You can imagine the fulfillment of each desire by running a mental movie, dramatizing and depicting the end, and your subconscious will bring it to pass.

9. You are always imagining, whether negatively or constructively. Imagine only what is lovely and of good report for yourself and also for others. Ask yourself, "Would I like to live with what I am picturing for the other?" Your answer should be "Yes." Remember that what you wish for the other, you are wishing for yourself.

10. Imagine that others are happy, joyous, rich, and affluent,

and rejoice in their prosperity and success. This is one sure way to acquire riches for yourself.

11. In the science of imagination, you eliminate all dross and impurities, such as covetousness, jealousy, envy, fear, doubt, and anger. Focus your attention only on your goals and imagine them fulfilled in Divine order.

12. Man is what he imagines himself to be. Imagine that which is lovely, noble, and God-like. Feel yourself as rich, and all the riches of Heaven will gravitate to you.

chapter 12

Be a Lifter and Grow Rich

THE Bible says, *And I, if I be lifted up from the earth, will draw all men unto me. (John 12:32.)*

This statement, like many others in the Bible, is purely psychological and spiritual, written in idiomatic, oriental language, telling all of us how to lift up ourselves from poverty, sickness, lack, and limitation of all kinds.

To be a lifter-upper, you must lift up your desires to the point of acceptance; then the manifestation will follow. Your physical senses report their findings, which at best are depressing. As a lifter-upper, you turn within to the Infinite Presence and Power, and anchor your mind there. This Infinite Presence is responsive to you, and when you call upon the Divine Power you will receive an answer. You can receive courage, faith, strength, power, and wisdom which transcend the ordinary physical senses. You are then lifted up, the old state dies, and the new state is resurrected.

You cannot manifest your good in a depressed state. Behold your vision and contemplate its reality, and you will rise above all obstacles, obstructions, and difficulties. As you contemplate the Presence of God within you, you will dissipate automatically all the fearsome shadows lurking in your mind.

You don't as a rule rise by accident from the slums and obscurity to wealth, honor, and fame by saving someone from drowning at the seashore or by meeting a millionaire who likes you. Remember a simple truth: You will always demonstrate your character, for character is destiny.

How to Rise to Great Heights

Release your energy, talents, and abilities, and develop a zeal and an enthusiasm to learn more about your inner powers. You then can lift yourself up to astonishingly great heights. An energetic, confident, and enterprising man who attends to business, does the right thing, and practices the golden rule will make a success of his life whether or not he meets a stranger who will help him, knows the right congressman, or wins a sweepstakes ticket.

Your character and mental attitude will make or break you. This is true of you, your country, your business, your church, or of any institution.

If you desire to lift up yourself and put your head above the ruck, ask God to give you what you need—and He will. You can build into your subconscious mind any quality you desire by meditating every day upon that quality.

The Joy of Overcoming

You are here to grow, to transcend, and to discover the Divinity within. You are here to meet problems, difficulties, and challenges—and then to overcome them. The joy is in the overcoming! If the crossword puzzle was filled out for you, it would be a very insipid and dull world. The engineer rejoices in overcoming all obstacles, failures, and difficulties in building his bridge. You are here to sharpen your mental and spiritual tools while you grow rich in wisdom, strength, and understanding; otherwise, you would never discover your Divinity.

Don't let your young boy lean on you indefinitely for everything. When he is old enough, teach him to mow the lawn, how to sell newspapers, and how to do well the odd jobs for which he is paid. Teach him the dignity of labor and that the money he receives from mowing the lawn for a neighbor or for selling newspapers is for work well done. This will give your young son pride in accomplishment and in his contribution in service to others. It will also teach him self-reliance and confidence in himself. Teach him also to see the good in others and how to call it forth, and he will always be a lifter and not a leaner, whiner, and complainer. He will respect and save the money he earns, but will put the easy money you give him into the juke box or the pool hall.

How to Lift Up Others

You must be careful of how you give to others. Never rob a man of his opportunity to grow and to advance. The young man who receives money and help too easily and too frequently finds it easier than self-discovery and self-propulsion. Constant assistance is destructive to his manhood. Cease emasculating and destroying his manly characteristics. Give him an opportunity to overcome and to discover his inner powers; otherwise, you will make him a leaner, always seeking a handout.

I told a woman to stop filling the ice box for a relative of hers who came from the East. Her attitude was: "Poor Tom, he is a stranger here. It's hard for him to get a job," etc. She paid his rent, bought groceries for him, and gave him pocket money until such time as he could get a job. He never got a job, but rather he became the perfect leaner—and he even resented her because she didn't give more! At a Christmas dinner to which he was invited he actually stole most of her silver. She cried out, "Why did he do this, after all I have done for him?"

She had been seeing him through the eyes of lack and limitation, however, and instead of lifting him up, realizing he was one with the Infinite and Divinely led to his true place; and clothing him mentally with the riches of Heaven, she had, figuratively speaking, clothed him in rags. He subconsciously picked this up and reacted accordingly.

You should always be ready to help a person who is really hungry or in want or distress. This is right, good, and true. However, be sure that you do not make a parasite of the other. Your assistance must always be based on Divine guidance and your motivation must be to help him to help himself. Teach the other where to find the riches of life and how to become self-reliant and how to contribute his best to humanity, and he will never want a bowl of soup, an old suit of clothes, or a handout.

. . . *These things . . . ye have done and . . . left the other undone. (Matthew 23:23.)* All of us are willing to give a helping hand, but it is wrong to contribute to the shortcomings, derelictions, laziness, apathy, and indifference of others.

Character Is Destiny

All of us are here to put our shoulders to the wheel. If you are wearing just a loin cloth, someone made it for you. What are you doing for others? Are you working and contributing your talents and abilities? There are many beggars who are able-bodied and who make a profession of begging for alms, and as long as you give to them they will never work. They become parasites and leaners. Some of them are very wealthy and have fashionable homes and cars, whether in London, New York, or elsewhere.

Within every man there is a vast mine of undiscovered gifts, powers, and riches. Each man is responsible, and boys must be made aware of their responsibilities to society. All of us are a part of humanity on the pathway of life. You are to do your share, whether pulling an oar or driving a car. Life rewards faith, courage, endurance, stick-to-it-iveness, and persistence with more of these qualities. It is in overcoming obstacles that you develop character, and character is destiny.

Your Inner Support

Lean on God and not on people or the government. The government can't give you anything unless it first takes it away from you. Furthermore, no government can legislate peace, harmony, joy, abundance, security, wisdom, love of neighbor, equality, prosperity, or goodwill. All these come from the spiritual world within you.

There is the leaner who drifts along on his name, background, heredity, or good looks until people become aware of how empty inside he is. Then he falls—he has no inner support and strength.

How He Rose to Fabulous Heights

A business executive in Los Angeles told me that in 1929 he had lost everything in the market crash. So did his brother. Each of them had been worth over a million dollars. His brother committed suicide; he said that there was nothing to live for, that he had lost everything.

This business executive told me he said to himself, "I have lost money; so what? I have good health, a lovely wife, abilities, and talents. I'll make it again. God will guide me and open up a new door for me. I am going to make millions." He rolled up his sleeves and went out as a gardener and did odd jobs here and there. He accumulated some money, invested it in stocks, and

saw them rise to fabulous heights. He gave advice to others, and
they made a small fortune.

He was a lifter. He had lifted up himself, for he knew there
is a God-Power which would reveal to him a way out, an answer.
He had called upon the spiritual reserves within him, and
strength, courage, wisdom, and guidance came to him.

The Riches of God Are Yours

The Bible says, *Draw nigh to God, and he will draw nigh to
you* ... (*James 4:8.*) All this means is that Infinite Intelligence
is responsive to you and will answer when you call. *I and my
Father are one.* (*John 10:30.*) You and God are one.

Don't lean on land, stocks, the government, relatives, or any-
body else. Trust the God-Power within to sustain you and to
watch over you at all times. Stop looking outside. Look inside.
If you look outside for help, you are denying the riches of God
within and you are stealing power, wisdom, and intelligence
from yourself.

Believe in yourself as a spiritual being of grandeur, and recognize your Divinity. Moreover, contemplate the truth that you are
here to release the imprisoned splendor that is within.

Be a lifter always by realizing that there is an Infinite Power
to back you up. This Power will lift you up, heal you, inspire
you, open up new doors for you, give you new creative ideas,
and present you with a sense of deep, abiding security in that
which changes not and is the same yesterday, today, and forever.
All you have to do is to trust this Presence and believe in It, and
wonders will happen in your life.

The lifter meets a problem head-on and he says to himself,
"This problem is Divinely outmatched. The problem is here, but
God is here, too." And he wins! He grapples with all hurdles,
business problems, and engineering and space problems with
faith, courage, and confidence, and he goes forth to conquer

sickness, fear, and ignorance. Man will never abolish the material slums until he abolishes the slums in the mind of man.

There is an old saying that the weak chick gets picked to death by the healthy ones. The boy in school who feels weak, defeated, rejected, bemeaned, and who is picked on by the bully and others, is also weak inside himself. But when he stands up to the bully, challenges him, and meets him head on, the so-called bully usually retreats.

You Can Rise Over All Conditions

Feel your dignity and grandeur as a son of God and realize that you are immune to insults, criticisms, and vilification by others because you are God-intoxicated. If you exalt and love the God-Presence within you, all men—even your so-called enemies—will be constrained to do you good.

Refuse to accept suffering and never resign yourself to any situation. You are a transcendental being and you can lift yourself up mentally over all conditions and circumstances.

When Abraham Lincoln was informed that a member of his Cabinet, the Secretary of War, was maligning and traducing him and calling him an ignorant baboon, he replied, "He is the greatest Secretary of War this country ever had." No one could hurt Lincoln or wound his ego. Lincoln knew where his strength was, and he knew that no one could drag him down except through a movement of his own mind. Lincoln was a lifter, which means that he not only lifted up himself but recognized the God-Self within him; he thereby acquired the strength to lift a whole country.

Be Nice to Yourself

You know of some so-called do-gooders who go about seeking paroles for molesters of children, sex-fiends, and other deviates

who, the minute they get out, again attack, rape, and even kill.
Our newspapers are full of this sort of thing. Before you can
uplift and help others, you must first be lifted up in wisdom and
understanding. You can give only what you have. Often, the
soap-box preachers and the do-gooders are simply projecting
their own shortcomings and inadequacies upon others. The
blind cannot lead the blind.

There is no one to change but yourself. You have to be nice to
yourself; the real Self of you is God. Exalt, honor, revere, and
respect this Divine Presence within yourself; then you are loving
and honoring your neighbor. Your neighbor is the closest thing
to you; God is your neighbor, and if you love God you will
have goodwill for all men.

> Speak to Him thou for He hears, and
> Spirit with Spirit can meet—
> Closer is He than breathing, and
> Nearer than hands and feet.

> Tennyson: *The Higher Pantheism* (Stanza 6)

Look at the reality of yourself, shining in all pristine glory
in your depths. Let your true Light shine, and let His love flow
through you, expu ing all your weaknesses, shortcomings, and
deficienci s. The l a has found God within himself and feels
strong an sec re j His Presence.

The lif er knows hat he is here to go forth conquering and
to conquer, for God or the Infinite cannot fail, and because he
is one with God, he has no fear and is no longer frustrated or
distrait.

Getting a New Estimate of Yourself

The lifter affirms, "God gave me this desire, and the God-
wisdom will reveal the perfect plan for its unfoldment." This
attitude dispenses with all frustration.

All of us are interdependent. You may need a doctor, a lawyer, a psychologist, or a carpenter—and they may need you. We need each other. But let us remember to lift up God in everyone and to see each man as he ought to be: a son of God, radiant, joyous, prosperous, and free.

Be a lifter. Exalt God in the midst of everyone. Clothe them with majesty and excellence and adorn and embellish them with the sunshine of His love. As you first exalt the Divinity within yourself, you will then exalt It also in others. Seek and you shall find tongues in trees, sermons in stones, songs in running brooks, and God in everything and in everybody.

The lifter knows the truth of this ancient saying: *What thou seest that, too, become thou must; God if thou seest God and dust if thou seest dust.*

As Moses lifted up the serpent in the wilderness, even so must the son of man be lifted up. The word *son* in the Bible means expression, and the word *man* means mind. All this means is that you must be a lifter-upper, like Moses, and when you are dejected, depressed, or fearful, lift up your concept of the Spirit within you which is God. You have a mind which is part of Infinite Mind; you have spirit within which at the human level is called feeling or emotion. In other words, the invisible part of you is God.

Cease crawling, cringing, and living in the shallows and eddies of life! Stop apologizing for being alive! Get a new estimate, a new blueprint of yourself. A serpent crawls on its belly and hides in caves or behind rocks away from the light. When you feel inadequate or weak and have a worm-of-the-dust attitude, you are crawling along the ground, governed by sense-evidence, and you feel that you are a victim of heredity, environment, and conditions. During the creative act, two serpents stand erect, which is symbolic of the caduceus worn by medical officers in the army. The serpent is thus a symbol of the Infinite Healing

Presence of God. This is to remind you to exalt and to lift up
the Healing Presence within yourself. The Father-Mother-God is
within you in the form of your conscious and subconscious mind.
Whatever you claim and feel to be true, your subconscious will
respond in like manner; hence, you can rise above all limitations,
impediments, and obstructions.

How to Experience the Joy of the Answered Prayer

In the Book of Numbers it says, *And Moses made a serpent
of brass, and put it upon a pole, and it came to pass, that if a
serpent had bitten any man, when he beheld the serpent of brass,
he lived. (Numbers 21:9.)*No intelligent person takes this story
literally. The Bible uses outer concrete things to portray inner
psychological and spiritual truths. Figuratively speaking, the
serpent bites you when you are full of hatred, jealousy, envy,
hostility, or vengeance. Many are bitten by covetousness and
enmity towards others because of their success and achievements
in life. Millions are bitten by fear, ignorance, and superstition.

Psychologically speaking, *Moses* means your awareness of the
Power of God and your capacity to draw it out from the depths
of yourself. Brass is an alloy of two metals, symbolic of the
union or agreement of your conscious and subconscious mind
regarding that for which you pray. If there is no quarrel or argu-
ment in your conscious or subconscious mind, your prayer will
be answered.

You are healed of all your infirmities when you gaze upon
the Infinite Healing Presence of God within you and claim that
what is true of God is true of you and of all men. Then you will
release the spiritual agencies on your behalf and you will ascend
from a crawling, cringing, creeping worm-of-the-dust attitude to
the exalted mood of faith and confidence in the joy of the Lord
which is your strength.

Be a lifter-upper from now on! The Spirit in you is God. It is invincible, invulnerable, eternal, almighty, and omniscient. Unite with this Presence and Power in your mind, feel the response, and your desert of loneliness, fear, sickness, poverty, and inferiority will rejoice and blossom as the rose. . . . *I bore you on eagles' wings, and brought you unto myself.* (*Exodus 19:4.*) It also brings you financial blessings for a fuller life.

CHAPTER SUMMARY

Higher Aspects of Living

.1 To be a lifter-upper you must lift up your desires to the point of acceptance; then the manifestation comes. Behold your vision and contemplate its reality.

2. Your character or mental attitude will make you or break you.

3. The two kinds of people on earth are the people who lift and the people who lean.

4. Lift the other up by realizing he is one with the infinite riches of Heaven and prospered beyond his fondest dreams.

5. Your character is destiny. Life rewards courage, faith, endurance, and persistence. It is in overcoming obstacles that you develop character.

6. The riches of God are yours because God or Infinite Intelligence is responsive to you and will answer when you call.

7. You can rise over all conditions by exalting the God-Presence within you and by uniting with It.

8. Be nice to yourself, because the real Self of you is God. Exalt God in the midst of you, and honor, revere, and respect the Divinity which is omniscient, omnipotent—the only Presence and the only Power.

9. Be a lifter and exalt God in the midst of everyone. First exalt the Divinity within yourself and you will then exalt it also in others.

10. Turn your eyes upwards and behold the infinite healing Presence within you, and as you feel the response you will experience the joy of the answered prayer. This includes financial blessings.

chapter 13

A Grateful Heart
Attracts Riches

LET *us come before his presence with thanksgiving.* (*Ps. 95:2.*)

The whole process of mental, spiritual and material riches may be summed up in one word, *gratitude.* A grateful thought for any good received is in itself a prayer from the heart and blesses you. A man with a grateful heart is a happy man and a wealthy man. Shakespeare said: "O Lord, who lends me life, lend me a heart replete with thankfulness."

Henry Thoreau, one of the wisest philosophers of America, said: "We should give thanks that we were born." Just consider for a moment if you had not been born. You would never have seen a glorious sunset or a beautiful sunrise. You would never have seen the lovely eyes of your child and the adoring eyes of your dog or his gaze upon his master. You would never have seen the beauties of nature or the starry heavens, the daily bread of the soul.

You would never have seen the snow-clad mountains scintillating like diamonds on a sunlit day. You would never have felt the affectionate embrace of your loved ones. You would never have seen the riches all around you or been able to smell the sweet fragrance of the flowers or the new mown hay.

Be thankful and grateful for the beauty of the morning. Be grateful you have eyes to see God's beauty, ears to hear the music of the spheres and the song of the birds, hands to play the melody of God, and a voice enabling you to speak words of comfort, courage and love to others.

Be grateful for your home, your loved ones, your relatives, your work and your business associates. Say frequently, "I bless and pray for every member of my family; I give thanks, I am grateful, I praise and I exalt God in my husband, my wife, and my children. I bless everything they are doing. I bless all the gifts I make. I know it is more blessed to give than to receive. I bless my business, I bless my co-workers, my customers, and all people. My work grows, expands, multiplies, increases and returns to me a thousandfold."

Law of Gratitude

First, you accept completely and wholeheartedly that there is an Infinite Intelligence from which all things flow; second, you believe that this Source responds to the nature of your thought; and third, you relate yourself to this Infinite Intelligence by a deep feeling of inner gratitude.

There is a law of gratitude and you must conform with the law in order to get results. This law as given in the Bible is, *Draw nigh unto God and He will draw nigh unto you.* This law is the natural principle of action and reaction which is cosmic and universal, or to elaborate and elucidate further, it simply means that whatever you impress on your subconscious mind will be expressed. The grateful attitude of your mind lifted up in thankful praise for the good that you share becomes a conviction in your deeper mind, resulting in the movement toward you of that which you claimed.

How Gratitude Draws Riches

An osteopath once told me how poor he had been as a boy and how he had worked as a janitor in order to pay his expenses through school. When he first opened his office, a whole week passed by and not one patient entered; he was bitter and critical. During the second week his first patient entered and said to him: "We are so grateful you opened up here; we needed you in our neighborhood. Several of us have prayed that you would be blessed and happy here," and then she added, "I am always so grateful for everything. I know that great numbers are kept in misery and poverty by their lack of gratitude."

This was the turning point in his life. Her words sank deeply into his heart, and he gave thanks for the healing power that was now flowing through him to this woman; he gave thanks for the fee she gave him. The more gratefully he fixed his mind on the Source of all healing and the good things he possessed, the more he received. His grateful attitude brought his whole mind in closer harmony with the creative forces of the universe, and patients flocked to him. He became rich in wisdom, had miraculous healings, and developed a very rich and influential practice.

Technique of Gratitude

A father promises a daughter a trip around the world, all expenses paid, as a gift following her graduation. She has not yet received the money for the trip, neither is she on the tour, but she is extremely grateful and happy and is as joyous as if actually on board ship bound for Europe and then the Orient. She knows her father will fulfill his promise and is very thankful, and she has mentally received the gift with a joyous anticipation and grateful heart.

You have probably gone to an automobile dealer and purchased a motor car, although they did not have exactly what you wanted in stock. You specified what you wanted, and the salesman said they would order it and deliver it. You thanked the salesman and walked away without the car. You were absolutely sure of receiving the motor car, exactly as ordered, in the near future because you trusted and believed in the integrity and honesty of the man who operated the business.

How much more should you trust in the Infinite and His creative law which never changes and which responds with absolute fidelity to our trust and belief in It!

Why Give Thanks?

. . . In everything give thanks. (1 Thess. 5:18.)

Primitive man had a childish concept of God and looked upon Him as an anthropomorphic being who ruled the universe tyranically and despotically, and he responded like the serfs and vassals who cringed and fawned before the old feudal lords who held the power of life and death over their people. Thus, primitive man similarly courted God's favor by prostrating himself, begging, beseeching, and fawning before Him.

Today, man looks at God as Infinite Intelligence, operating through creative law. This law is impersonal, is no respecter of persons and changes not; it is the same yesterday, today and forever. The Divine Presence also has all the elements of personality such as love, joy, peace, wisdom, intelligence and harmony, and It becomes personal and intimate with the man who tunes in and operates the law righteously. When man discovers the wonders, glories and responsiveness of the Infinite Presence and Power, there immediately arises within him praise, gratitude and exultation of his spirit, just as when the young boy discovers some secret of chemistry or nature, he is thrilled and happily tells his father all about this discovery. The boy's tendency is to exult and seek praise at his findings. A little boy of ten presented me with an ashtray which he had made himself in school. He explained how he had machined the metals and soldered them together, and you could see the thrill and wonder of it all in his eyes. This will induce the boy to seek out more and more secrets in the school laboratory. Praise and gratitude do not move God or the Law, but it brings about a transformation in our mind and heart and becomes a spiritual and mental magnet attracting all kinds of good, including money, to us from countless sources.

Your gratitude, your praise, and your measure of thankfulness must not be expressed as a fawning or cringing attitude seeking favors. Instead it should be a thrilling adventure into the recesses of your deeper mind where you review and become intensely interested in the laws of God. Herein you will rejoice that all things you need and claim are within you in principle, and they wait for you to receive them with a joyful and thankful heart.

You are truly grateful and have a heart full of praise when you become aware of and appreciate the universal principles of life and the Providence which gave you everything from the foundation of time. "All things be ready if the mind be so." (Shakespeare)

The Miracle of "Thank You"

A man said, "Bills are piling up, I have no money, I must go into bankruptcy. What shall I do?" I suggested that for ten or fifteen minutes two or three times a day, he sit down quietly and affirm boldly, "Thank you, Father, for thy riches now," and to continue in that relaxed and peaceful manner until the feeling or mood of thankfulness dominated his mind. He knew that the thought-image of wealth was the first cause relative to the money and riches he needed. His thought-feeling was the substance of wealth untrammeled by previous conditioning of any kind.

By repeating, "Thank you, Father," over and over again, his mind and heart were lifted up to the point of acceptance, and when fear thoughts came to his mind, he would immediately say, "Thank you, Father," as often as necessary. He knew that as he kept up this grateful attitude he would recondition his mind to the idea of wealth, which is exactly what happened. He met a former employer at a social gathering who offered him an executive position and also advanced him a considerable sum of money which enabled him to pay off all bills and be free of debt. He remarked to me that he would never forget the wonders of "Thank you, Father."

Value of Gratitude

Gratitude keeps you in tune with the Infinite and connected with the creative law. The value of gratitude does not consist purely in drawing to you many blessings. You must remember that without the thankful heart you become dissatisfied and disgruntled regarding your present condition and circumstances.

If you fix your attention on poverty, lack, loneliness, squalor, meanness, and the difficulties and problems of the world, your mind takes the form of all these things, based upon the law that that to which you give attention, you also experience.

Remember, if you allow your mind to dwell on lack and limitation you will surround yourself with misery and inferior things.

Fix your attention on the highest and the best in life and you will experience and surround yourself similarly with the highest and best of everything in life.

The creative law of your subconscious mind makes you into

the image and likeness of that which you contemplate. Actually you become what you contemplate. The grateful man continually and invariably expects the good things of life and his expectation inevitably takes material form.

It is necessary and essential to adopt the habit of being grateful for all the good you receive; in other words, give thanks continually.

All men contribute to your well being. You should therefore include all men and women in your prayer of gratitude. This will bring you into subconscious communication with the good in all men and in everything, and the riches of life, the earth and all men will gravitate automatically toward you.

Do You Appreciate Your Good?

Some years ago I read in the local newspaper about a man who had been blind since he was two years old. One eye had to be removed, but later on doctors operated on the other eye, and the first thing he saw was the face of his wife. To him she was extremely beautiful and he could not imagine anything more wonderful. He had lived with her for nearly forty years and had never seen her face. Do you appreciate your wife, your husband, your family, your boss? Do you give thanks for your eyes, your body and your confidence of faith in God and all things good?

The Riches of Forgiveness

Last Christmas I chatted with a man who told me that he had not written or communicated with his parents in twenty years— he had had a misunderstanding, had felt they gave more money and property to his brother than to him, and remained angry and vindictive. His two assistants in the shop said, "You know all the workers here are going home to visit their parents Christmas

Day; it must be wonderful to have parents. My, how we would love to have that opportunity on Christmas. We are orphans; we never knew our parents. It must be wonderful to have parents." This man was deeply touched and instantaneously his anger and his hostility toward his parents melted and he went home for Christmas with gifts for his father and mother, and there was a joyous reunion. As a gift his parents turned over some valuable stocks to him which far exceeded in value the amount he imagined he had been deprived of in relation to his brother.

Forgiveness is giving—giving love, peace, and all the blessings of life to the other—and as you give, you receive. It is written: *It is more blessed to give than to receive.*

Gratitude Attracts Fifty Million Dollars

This is a marvelous story of the power of the grateful heart. The young man's name was Lucien Hamilton Tyng. He was born in Peoria, Illinois, which offered very little for the ambitions of this young man who dreamed big dreams and thought big and expansively. Lucien decided to go to Chicago and try his luck. He got a job as office boy which barely paid him a living wage; after his room rent was paid, it left him exactly fifty cents a day for meals. He found that a five cent bag of chocolate cream made a very filling lunch. Breakfast was fifteen cents, so dinner could not be more than thirty-five cents. He was very religious; he made it a constant habit to hold his fifty cent piece in his hand and say: "God multiplies this and I give thanks. I am receiving more and more money everyday." He would repeat this for about ten minutes every morning before he spent the fifty cents. He began to attract many clever and successful men, and opportunities began to arrive his way which he was quick to take advantage of. "Thank you, Father," was constantly on his lips. As the years passed many influential men began to ask his opinion and were guided by it. He seemed to be miraculously gifted, his mental acumen gradually increased. His sagacity in business was admired by other men and he was deeply trusted. He solved many business problems for them. His constant prayer was "Thank you, Father," before and after every successful achievement.

One day a wonderful idea came to him, which he related to a good friend who said it had tremendous potentialities. They formed a partnership and incorporated what was then called the "General Gas and Electric Company." It grew by leaps and bounds with stations all over the Eastern states, and after many years they sold it for a reported sum of fifty million dollars.

A poet once said: "Oh, God, give me one more thing—a grateful heart."

CHAPTER SUMMARY

Steps to Riches

1. The whole process of mental, spiritual and material riches may be summed up in one word, *gratitude*.
2. There is a law of gratitude and you must conform with the law to gain results. It simply means that whatever you impress in your subconscious likewise will be expressed. Rejoice and give thanks for wealth and all kinds of riches, and by feeling rich you will so impress your deeper mind and riches will be yours.
3. Give thanks for what you now possess and for your many blessings. Count these one by one and God will multiply your good exceedingly.
4. Give constant praise and be thankful for your knowledge of the creative laws which bring all kinds of riches in your

life. You are grateful for the car promised by your father but not yet received. Your Heavenly Father will give you much more. All He needs is your complete trust and faith in Him.

5. Look on God as Infinite Mind and Infinite Intelligence operating through a creative law which responds to all and is no respecter of persons. When you discover the riches and glories within you, you can't help but exult with praise and gladness in discovery that all things you seek exist in principle and wait for you to receive them with a joyful and thankful heart.

6. Sit down for fifteen minutes every day, quiet your mind and affirm: "Thank you, Father, for Thy riches now," and wonders including those of money, will happen in your life.

7. Gratitude keeps you in tune with the Infinite and connected with the creative forces of the universe; and you become a mental and spiritual magnet attracting countless blessings.

8. Show your deep appreciation for those around you, members of your family and your co-workers. People crave appreciation. Give it freely and lovingly.

9. Forgiveness creates a vacuum in your mind, leaving way for the Infinite Healing Presence to flow through you. Many do not grow rich because of their criticism, resentment and hostility to others. This attitude cuts the wires which bind you with the Source of all wealth and all health. Bless others until there is no sting in your heart.

10. If you have only a dollar in your pocket, bless it by saying, "God multiplies this money exceedingly in my experience and I am grateful for the constantly increasing, tireless flow of God's riches in life." You will attract fantastic wealth.

11. *I thank Thee, Father, that Thou hast heard me and I know that Thou hearest me always. (John 17:24.)*

chapter 14

Miracles of Riches Through the Power of Your Words

DID you ever think of the marvelous power of words? To think is to speak. Your thought is your word. The Bible says, in the *Book of Proverbs (25:11.)*, *A word fitly spoken is like apples of gold in pictures of silver.* We are also instructed as follows: *Pleasant words are as an honeycomb, sweet to the soul, and health to the bones. (Proverbs 16:24.)*

Are your words sweet to the ear? If you say, "I can't get ahead. It is impossible. I'm too old now. What chance have I to be rich? Mary can, but I can't. I have no money; I can't afford this or that. I've tried; it's no use," you can see that your words are not as a honeycomb; they are not constructive. They do not lift you up or inspire you. Furthermore, what you decree in words will actually come to pass.

The words you speak must be pleasant to the *bones*, which means that your speech must exalt you, thrill you, and make you happy. *Bones* are symbolic of support and symmetry. Your speech must sustain and strengthen you. Decree now, and say it meaningfully: "From this moment forward, the words which I use will heal, bless, prosper, inspire, and strengthen me and everybody else."

Since your words literally are so powerful, it is important to say the right thing at the right time and, furthermore, to be sure that your words on all occasions are "sweet to the ear and pleasant to the bones."

Dr. Phineas Parkhurst Quimby of Maine pointed out over a hundred years ago that primitive man desired to communicate his hopes, aspirations, longings, likes, dislikes, and fears. He had an intense desire to communicate these thoughts and feelings to his fellow man. This was first evidenced by grunts and groans, and finally resulted in the formation of root words. From these, he added to his vocabulary to coincide with his mental and spiritual development.

Following this capacity to articulate his thoughts and feelings came, ultimately, the printing press, printed words, the typewriter, and countless other modern inventions to propagate knowledge in the form of words all over the world. Marconi decided to send his word around the world; his relatives thought he was psychotic and had him incarcerated for a while in an insane asylum. Nevertheless, his idea brought forth a new dimension in communication, and today we collapse time and space through his idea. You can pick up a phone today and talk to someone at the ends of the earth!

Begin to realize the wonders of speech and how you can bless, exalt, prosper, and inspire all those with whom you communicate.

Using Words with Authority

Word power is greater than thermo-nuclear weapons or atomic bombs, for the simple reason that words decree whether these weapons are to be used or remain latent. Words may be used to order atomic power to drive a ship across an ocean or to devastate a city or a nation.

Solomon said: ... *The tongue of the wise is health.* (*Proverbs 12:18.*) And again: *Death and life are in the power of the tongue* ... (*Proverbs 18:21.*) Here is the key to using words with authority.

I recited these words to a man who was in the hospital with cardiac trouble, and he began to say to himself the greater part of the day: "I am all health; God is my health." To the astonishment of his cardiologist, he had a most remarkable recovery. Another cardiograph was taken, revealing a normal heart. He used words with authority and conviction, and they found their way to his subconscious mind which responded accordingly.

He said to me, "Health is wealth. Now I can go back to my family and my business who need me, and finish educating my children."

His Words Brought Him Riches

I once had an interview with a business man, and he said that the key to his prosperity and success in the business world was his constant realization of the truth behind these words: ... *The words that I speak ... are spirit, and they are life.* (*John 6:63.*)

He said, "My riches and blessings have been brought about by these words and the manner in which I spoke them. I poured my deepest feeling (spirit) into these words. I knew my feeling was the real evidence of the spirit behind them and which alone gave them creative substance."

This man has accomplished great things in the business world and has proved to himself that riches result from the right word spoken in the right way.

How the Authority of Words Can Bless

A real estate broker told me the secret of his capacity to take control and to issue decrees to his subconscious mind. His words of command are: "My words heal, quicken, vitalize, prosper, satisfy, and make rich all those whom I contact or do business with." His attitude is that the more life, love, goodwill, and riches he passes on to others, the more he possesses. Niagara is mighty because it pours forth freely.

This broker is immensely popular and very successful. He believes that what you decree you receive, as the Bible promises: *Thou shalt decree a thing, and it shall be established unto thee: and the light shall shine upon thy ways. (Job 22:28.)*

How Living Word Was Made Flesh

Once I tried to help a man who had suffered financial reverses. I noticed that he was constantly saying, "If I could get my hands on some money, I'd be all right." I explained to him that he had to account for every idle word he spoke and that his subconscious does not take a joke, but accepts literally what he decrees. His hands were constantly shaking, and the words which he was using indicated doubt and anxiety and kept him financially on a merry-go-round.

He began to use the transforming power of the living word, so that it "became flesh," or was made manifest. He then declared frequently: "I decree wealth and success, and I know that these words sink down into my subconscious because I say them meaningfully and sincerely. I am financially secure, and in my hands is all the money I need, and I give thanks."

Soon he turned the tide, both in his hands and financially! *And the Word was made flesh, and dwelt among us ... (John 1:14.)*

The Living Word Works Wonders

The concept which is faithfully held in your mind and heart is made flesh, in accordance with the quality and the nature of your words. Words are the mental equivalents which produce their image and likeness not only in our bodies, but in all our environment, relationships, and affairs.

Dr. Olive Gaze, an associate of mine, constantly uses the power of the word to enrich others. She verbally affirms (which means to fix in your mind, to make firm and real) whatever good it is that the person wants. When someone is seeking supply or more money, she affirms for them frequently during the day: "God is rich. Mary is God's child, and she is rich now. It is so!" This simple method brings forth rich results to all those who call upon her. These words have worked wonders in the lives of many.

How Words Command Miracle Power

Jesus, at the tomb of Lazarus, commanded the miracle power and decreed out loud: *Lazarus, come forth. (John 11:43.)* And the resurrected man came forth to greet his sister and his friend, Jesus, who had spoken with authority. . . . *He spoke to them as one having authority . . . (Matthew 7:29.)*

Become entranced and fascinated by the power of your words! Never use words of lack, limitation, discord, or bad times; but begin to build a new body and a new environment, plus mental and material riches by changing your words of command. Affirm boldly: "Wealth, come forth! Health, come forth! Success, come forth!" and you will experience the joy of the answered prayer.

How Words Attracted Clients

The people who attended my prosperity class on "The Amazing Laws of Cosmic Mind Power"[1] found that the power of

---

[1] See *The Amazing Laws of Cosmic Mind Power*, by Joseph Murphy, published by Parker Publishing Company, Inc., West Nyack, © 1965.

words would produce fabulous results for them. I suggested that they take certain words which appealed to them and verbally decree them over and over for about ten or more minutes twice daily. Many told me that they worked in offices and could not always affirm out loud, so they wrote down what they were wishing to bring to pass and mentally went over their statements from time to time, thereby gradually conveying the ideas to their subconscious mind.

One of the men, who sells insurance, claimed boldly: "I am now attracting only those men and women who are interested and who have the money to invest for their children's education and for their own welfare." His persistent use of these affirmative words has attracted to him more interested people than ever before. Leads now come to him seemingly from nowhere, and he has made tremendous strides on the scale of life and in all its varied phases.

Remember—the power of words is one of the greatest gifts that God has bestowed on man. Animals can't talk or laugh. You must realize that you can use your words to bless or to curse, to heal or to make sick, to produce riches or poverty, for your betterment or for your detriment. Cease using the power of your words against yourself. Always bless, and then you will gather orchids in life, instead of thistles.

Her Words Settled an Inheritance Claim

A woman in San Francisco, an old friend of the author, phoned me some time ago and said that her father had not included her in his will, which was being probated, but that the estate was being divided equally among the other five members of her family, namely, her brothers and sisters. She consulted an attorney at my suggestion, and she affirmed these words for fifteen minutes, three or four times a day: "There is a Divine, harmonious adjustment to the estate, and that which is mine by

Divine right comes to me. I bless my sisters and my brothers, they bless me, and there is a happy ending."

After a week or so, her attorney called her and said that her brothers and sisters did not want her to contest the will and that they felt their father had been unfair to her because she had married a person of a different faith. They felt that it was none of their father's business whom she had married, and they had agreed to give her an equal share of the estate. There truly was a harmonious legal adjustment which resulted in an equal financial division for each one.

Your Healing Words

"Words are the most powerful drug used by mankind." (Rudyard Kipling.) The Bible says: *He sent his word, and healed them* . . . (*Psalm 107:20*.)

Every one of us can use healing words for ourselves and also for others. The reason we may not get immediate results is due to the nature of our faith or belief. Now, this is how to use healing words for another; it might be for a loved one or for a friend.

Feel the Presence of God, which is the presence of harmony, health, and peace, in your friend, going through him and around him; feel that he is Divinely watched over. Even though the other person may not know about it, you personally accept that the healing is taking place now, and you sincerely believe it. You can do this several times a day, if you wish. Your faith grows. The healing may come slowly or it may come quickly, according to your belief. That is "sending your word," which is your thought and feeling, to the other person.

The prophet Isaiah said, *The Lord God hath given me the tongue of the learned, that I should know how to speak a word in season to him that is weary* . . . (*Isaiah 50:4*.) A word of exaltation, of praise, of love; who can measure its power?

A dull boy could not learn; his teachers said that he was hopeless. His mother, though, was rich and powerful in love and faith, and she frequently affirmed during the day: "God loves my boy and He careth for him. The Intelligence of God wells up within him; the Wisdom of God is working through him; he is a perfect expression of God."

This boy is now normal, and he is doing very well at school. These are the spiritual riches of your words, when they are filled with love and understanding. Her words had power to harmonize and to heal.

His Words Caused Them to Pay

The credit manager of an engineering firm had many delinquent accounts, totaling nearly $30,000. He made a list of the past-due accounts, and every morning before he started to work he mentioned each name and spoke the words as follows: "John Doe is prospered and blessed, and his good is multiplied. He pays all his obligations promptly, and he is honest, sincere, and just. I give thanks now for his check. He is blessed; we are blessed. I give thanks that it is so."

This statement, or command, to his deeper mind reached each one of his customers who had been very lax, and all paid up within one month! His words of faith and trust were accepted by his subconscious mind and were telepathically received by those men who had been in arrears and who had previously failed to answer his frequent requests for payment.

How Her Words Opened a New Door for Employment

A woman, aged sixty, claimed that she could not find work and that all doors were closed to her because of her age. She affirmed as follows: "I am a child of God. I am always gainfully employed by my Father who is God, and my Father pays me handsomely and opens a new door for me."

She gained new strength and confidence, which were immediately apparent in her bearing, and she visited several agencies and made inquiries. In no time she found a wonderful position with an employer who was delighted to have her because of her stability, loyalty, and wisdom garnered through the years.

Your Words Can Solve Your Problems

A young secretary worked for a demanding individual who was somewhat sadistic in his language. She affirmed to herself as follows: "There is no man like this in the universe. God thinks, speaks, and acts through my employer. God is in him and speaks and acts through him."

Shortly afterwards, the employer turned the business over to his son, who shortly fell in love with the secretary. The author is happy to say that he had the pleasure of performing their marriage ceremony. This young woman had taken command of her words, and she found a Divine answer.

When you speak from the standpoint of the Infinite, your words are true; they have power, and they come to pass. *In the beginning was the Word, and the Word was with God, and the Word was God. (John 1:1.)*

CHAPTER SUMMARY

Rehearse These Truths

1. Your thought is your word. Words represent the armory of your mind. Thoughts are things, and your words come to pass.

2. Your words are far more powerful than atomic or nuclear energy. Words may be used to employ atomic power in the healing arts or to drive a ship across an ocean, or words may cause these same energies to be used destructively.

3. Let your words be full of spirit (feeling), and pour into them life and meaning, and you will experience the result in forms, functions, experiences, and events.

4. You can issue words of command, such as "My words heal, quicken, vitalize, prosper, satisfy, and make rich all those with whom I do business." These words will cause your business to flourish and to prosper. Your words are the body of your thought.

5. *Man shall decree a thing and it shall come to pass.* (*Job 22:28.*) In other words, your word "becomes flesh," or takes form in your world.

6. Your words are the mental equivalent which produce their image and likeness in your experience.

7. Learn to speak as one having authority. Believe implicitly that your subconscious answers your word, which is your conviction.

8. Use words which appeal to you, which fascinate and enthrall you, and repeat them frequently. It is the frequent habitation of the mind with these thoughts that produces miracles in your life.

9. Let your words flow from the standpoint of God and Truth, and you will find a harmonious adjustment in legal and other troublesome matters.

10. Rudyard Kipling said, "Words are the most powerful drug used by mankind." Your thought and feeling are your "word," which can heal not only yourself but also others. Think of the Presence of God, and become sincerely interested. You will rise in consciousness, and, according to your

rise in consciousness, a healing will follow. You can sharpen a dull child in this way.

11. Your words can cause customers who are delinquent in their payments to pay up. Bless them and they will feel it subconsciously and act accordingly.

12. If you are looking for employment, use these words feelingly and knowingly: "I am a child of God, and God is my employer. I am always gainfully employed, and I give thanks now for my perfect expression in life and for my wonderful income."

13. If another person speaks harshly to you or is sadistic in his language, affirm boldly that God indwells him and that there is no man like that in the universe; know that God is All, and God thinks, speaks, and acts through him. Feel the truth of this, and you will experience the joy of the answered prayer.

chapter 15

The Marvelous Riches
of the Silence

THE Silence is the rest of the mind in God, and as sleep nourishes and refreshes the body, so does communion with God nourish, sustain, and revitalize man. Emerson said, "Let us be silent that we may hear the whispers of the gods."

The Silence consists of withdrawing your attention and sensory awareness from the external world and then focusing your attention on your ideal, goal, or objective, while knowing that the Infinite Intelligence of your subconscious mind will inevitably respond and reveal the answer.

A Genius in Every Man

You came into the world with all the powers and qualities of God and the power to think as an individual. You think, therefore you have the power to create and to project your mental acceptances and beliefs into the world about you. You are rich when you are aware of your creative force. Your riches and even your security itself lie in your power to create.

While visiting a movie studio, I asked a motion picture writer, "How do you do the work? What do you do when you write a play?" He replied somewhat like this: "I quiet my mind, relax and let go. I just know what the idea of the script is. I think about the idea and enjoy it; then in the silence at night prior to sleep, I dwell upon the book, knowing that the theme, the characters, and the ideas will be given to me. In the morning when I wake up, I have the whole script, and I sit down and write it."

Now where did the play originate but in the mind of the writer? The ideas he entertained and meditated upon in the silence of the night were impressed upon his subconscious mind, and the latter automatically responded with all the creative ideas necessary for the book.

You live in your mind, and it is there that you become rich or poor, a beggar or a thief. You possess the pearl of great price when you know the power of your own thoughts to create what you want in life. The riches and the powers within you can never be depleted. The riches of your mind know no limitation but that which you impose upon yourself.

How He Drew Wealth from the Silence

Robert Louis Stevenson practiced the Silence regularly and systematically. He had the persistent habit of giving specific instructions to his subconscious mind in the silence of the night prior to sleep. With his attention withdrawn from the sense world around about him and turning inward to the wisdom and power of his subconscious mind, he would request his deeper mind to evolve stories for him while he slept. For example, if Stevenson's funds were at a low ebb, his command to his subconscious would be something like this: "Give me a good, thrilling novel which will be marketable and profitable." His subconscious mind responded magnificently.

Stevenson said, "These little brownies (the intelligence and powers of his subconscious mind) can tell me a story piece by piece like a serial and keep me, its supposed creator, all the while in total ignorance of where they aim." And he added, "that part of my work which is done when I am up and about is by no means necessarily mine, since all goes to show that the brownies have a hand in its existence."

His Silent Period Made Him Famous

Kahlil Gibran, who wrote *The Prophet,* not only deliberated in the silence of the night, communing with the God-Self within him, radiating love, peace, joy, and goodwill to all, but daily contemplated the inner radiance, light, love, truth and beauty within him, and he bequeathed to humanity the wealth of his meditations in the silences with God. Gibran turned frequently within to the One, the Beautiful, and the Good, and wrote, "A seeker of *Silences* am I and what treasures have I found in *Silences* that I may dispense with confidence."

He drew wisdom, truth and beauty from the ever-lasting fountain of living waters within. In the silence of the night and in tune with the Infinite he was inspired from on High and wrote majestic gems of wisdom, which made him famous, and also quite wealthy.

A Thrilling Experiment in the Silence

My tailor told me of a thrilling business experiment conducted by his daughter. She was going to model in a fashion show in New York and remarked to her father, "I saw a beautiful ermine coat in the show today for eight thousand dollars. I know we can't afford it, but I am going to perform an experiment in my mind. Oh, how I want it!"

Her father told her to imagine she was wearing the coat, to

feel its beautiful fur, and to get the feel of it on her. She practiced mentally putting on the imaginary coat. She fondled it and caressed it like a child does her doll. She continued to do this and finally felt the thrill of it all. In the silence of each night she went to sleep "wearing" the imaginary coat and feeling happy in possessing it. A month went by and nothing happened. She was about to waver, but she reminded herself that it is the sustained mood which demonstrates *He who perseveres to the end will be saved.* (*Matt. 10:22.*)

The sequel to her mental drama was that, ultimately, one Sunday morning after my lecture, a man accidentally stepped on her toe, apologized profusely, asked her where she lived and offered to drive her home. She accepted gladly. After a short acquaintanceship, he proposed marriage, gave her a beautiful diamond ring, and said to her, "I saw the most beautiful coat; you would look simply radiant wearing it." It was the coat she had admired a month previously. (The salesman said that many wealthy women had looked at the coat and had admired it immensely, but for some reason, they always selected another garment.)

How a Mother Recharged Her Emotions

A woman complained to me that her children were driving her crazy. I suggested to her that every morning she set aside about fifteen minutes and read the 91st and 23rd *Psalms* out loud, then close her eyes and detach herself from her surroundings. She was to think of God's Infinite love, boundless wisdom, supreme power, and absolute harmony, and feel the atmosphere of love, peace, joy and happiness surrounding and enfolding her children, claiming at the same time that His love and His peace filled her mind and heart and that the children were growing in peace, beauty, wisdom and understanding.

She recharged her mental and spiritual batteries with the power and the wisdom of God, and her whole life was transformed. Her love for her children grew by leaps and bounds. This is also the riches of peace she found in the Silence.

How a Pilot Practices the Silence

As a violent storm accompanied by thunder and lightning encircled the plane on which I was travelling to the Orient, the pilot told me that whenever he encounters a storm, he quietly recites the 23rd *Psalm,* adding, "God's love surrounds this plane and I bring it down in Divine order."

I noticed that at first, while the passengers were panicky, suddenly a great calm came over them. Our pilot made a perfect landing at Hong Kong and no one was hurt. He had refused to panic, thereby releasing the healing currents of love and protection for all.

He Solved His Problem in the Silence

A man complained bitterly to me that he could not get a job because he did not have a union card. Furthermore, he did not have the money to join the union. He wanted to send his son to college and to purchase a new home, but he said, "I'm frustrated at every step."

I said to him that he should listen to the true voice within himself. He had been looking at the negative aspect of things, but faith comes through hearing the eternal Truths of God. At night he became still, immobilized his attention, and affirmed, "Infinite Intelligence opens up a door of expression for me where I am Divinely happy and Divinely prospered. God opens up the way for my boy to go to college and God's wealth flows to me in avalanches of abundance."

A few days passed and he met a former employer, who immediately engaged him at a very high salary, and who turned over his own cottage near the plant for this man and his wife. With the increase in salary he was able to send his son to college. The answer came from the depths of himself as he quietly contemplated God's love and beneficence in the silence of the night.

How to Get Thrilling Results

Close the door of your senses, then you are no longer distracted by sense perceptions of the world, and silently dwell on the presence of God within you. You should go into His Presence in a joyful, receptive, and expectant attitude, knowing that Infinite Intelligence will respond when you call. When you go to the pond or fountain for water, you take a bucket or some other proper receptacle in which to receive the water. Likewise, when you tune in with the Infinite your receptive mind (the receptacle) will be filled with the Infinite Healing Presence and all the gifts of God.

You can begin now to enter the Silence periodically by simply reordering your mind, wherein you withdraw your attention from the diversity of sense evidence and commune with the indwelling God filling your soul with His love.

How to Lead a Charmed Life

A young doctor told me that as he studied the pathology of diseases he contracted several of the conditions he had studied. He realized that he was constantly involved in the morbid images and that his mind created what he had feared.

On realizing the cause of his predicament, however, he reversed the situation by contemplating that all diseases were due to distorted mental patterns on the part of patients. He began to contemplate the perfect pattern of harmony, health and peace. As he looked at the negative condition, he contemplated wholeness, beauty, and perfection. He began to see the presence of God in all patients, and he thereby became immunized against all disease.

He is now leading a charmed life. He goes into isolation wards, visits diseased patients, and is completely immunized.

A Scientist and the Silence

A famous engineer and space scientist, when presented with problems, sits alone in his research office and silently contemplates as follows: "I am being made aware of the Divine solution now. God knows the answer and I and my Father are one. God reveals it to me this instant."

He says that invariably and inevitably he receives the answer, sometimes as an intuitive flash in his mind which presents him with the necessary idea, or, often as a graph in his mind, which is the perfect answer. He likes to call his technique the "silent solution."

Why Nothing Happened

A woman said to me that she spent one-half hour in the Silence every day but got no results. I discovered that her procedure was to listen to music, have incense burning, and concentrate on statues of holy men. She also adopted certain postures, lit candles, erected altars in her home, and faced the East when she prayed.

Actually, she was completely involved in the periphery of life and externalities. Her whole life was chaotic. She was sick, frustrated, lonesome, bored, and suffered from various mental aberrations. Her mind was focused on statues, candles, rituals, incense, music and postures, all of which resulted in a sort of auto-hypnotic trance. She was impregnated by her five senses and was not communing with the Divine Presence at all.

Her sister was non-religious and was constantly chiding her, saying, "You pray every day and what good does it do you? Look at me. I don't go into the silence at all and I don't even believe in God, yet I am strong, vital and prosperous." Actually, this woman was not in the Silence at all. She was being impressed by sights, sounds, and statues and was simply wasting her energy and time on externalities. I explained to her the wise silence of Emerson, which she began to practice, resulting in a tremendous change in her mind, body and financial situation.

The Wise Silence of Emerson

Practice the wise Silence by turning away from the world and the evidence of your senses and contemplate the reality of your ideas or desires. "Believe you have it now and you shall receive it." This means that your desire, idea, plan, purpose or invention is as real as your hand or your heart. It has form, shape and substance in another dimension of mind.

Give it your attention, exult in it, know that Infinite Intelligence which gave you the idea will reveal the perfect plan for its unfoldment. Sustain this attitude and you will experience the joy of the answered prayer. This is the wise silence of Emerson.

Begin to Reap Rich Dividends Daily

Every morning when you arise, think of God and of His love and become alert and quickened with great expectancy, interest, and vital attention. Affirm quietly and slowly, "Into the Holy Omnipresence of God I give myself, my plans, my ideas, and all the affairs of my life this day. I dwell in the secret place of the

Most High, and His overshadowing Presence watches over me, my family, my business and all things appertaining to me. God walks and talks in me and wherever I go God and His love accompany me. God prospers me in all my undertakings and His wealth flows to me freely, joyously, endlessly and ceaselessly. I walk the earth with the praise of God forever on my lips."

As you practice the above method you will reap rich dividends in all departments of your life.

That Inner Stillness

"Let us then labor for an inward stillness—a stillness and an inward healing—that perfect silence where the lips and the heart are still and we no longer entertain our own imperfect thoughts and vain opinions, but where God alone speaks in us and we wait in singleness of heart that we may know His will and in the *Silence* of our spirit that we do His will and do that only." (Longfellow)

CHAPTER SUMMARY

Ideas Worth Remembering

1. The Silence is the rest of the mind in God, whereby we receive nourishment, vitality, and new strength.

2. There is a genius in every man. All the powers of God are within man waiting to be drawn forth by the conscious mind when it is stilled.

3. You may give specific instructions to your subconscious mind silently and lovingly prior to sleep and your subconscious will perform magnificently according to the nature of your directions.

4. You can draw forth marvelous ideas for a book, play or music from your deeper mind by stilling your conscious

mind prior to sleep and calling on the Infinite to reveal to you what you need to know.

5. In your business, take ten or fifteen minutes every morning and claim Infinite Intelligence is directing all your activities and that your payments, decisions and purchases will be governed and conditioned by the wisdom of God. Your business will prosper in a magnificent way.

6. If you can't afford an expensive coat, imagine that you have it on, feel its texture and beauty, fondle and caress it, and continue to wear it mentally, and you will receive it in ways you know not of.

7. You can recharge your mental and spiritual batteries in the Silence by slowly and quietly affirming the *91st* and *23rd Psalms* and knowing God's peace flows through your mind and heals.

8. In a storm at sea or in the air, quietly know God's love surrounds, enfolds, and enwraps you, and you will be at peace.

9. Go into the Silence with a feeling of great expectancy and vital attention and you will receive the gifts of God, all the riches of Heaven, and earthly riches as well.

10. Lead a charmed life by seeing the presence of God where discord, sickness or contagious disease and financial lack are present and you will build up an immunity to all these unharmonious conditions.

11. Claim that God has the answer and that you are one with God; therefore, you also have the answer and you will receive the Divine Solution to all problems.

12. In the Silence you detach yourself mentally from all external sights, sounds and objects and instead contemplate the reality of the wish fulfilled. As you do this, the power of God backs you up and you experience the joy of the answered prayer.